PREPARING FOR EMERGENCIES

PRESENTED TO: _____

ON: _____

MESSAGE:_____

_____

_____

_____

_____

_____

_____

_____

_____

_____

_____

_____

_____

PRESENTED BY: _____

PREPARING
· FOR ·
EMERGENCIES

DISASTER can strike YOU suddenly!

DR. JAMES McKEEVER
WITH
MRS. JEANI McKEEVER

PREPARING FOR EMERGENCIES

Copyright © 1993 by James M. McKeever
Copyright © 1998 by Jeani McKeever-Harroun

Printed in the United States of America
First printing August, 1993
Second printing October, 1998

Omega Publications
P. O. Box 4130
Medford, Oregon 97501 (U.S.A.)

ISBN #0-86694-125-8 (Softback)

TABLE OF CONTENTS

THIS BOOK IS DEDICATED TO SOME VERY SPECIAL PEOPLE IN OUR LIVES:

Jim and Pat Burck
Terry and Jayne Calkin
Giff and Winnie Claiborne
Rick Godwin
Stuart and Mary Gramenz
Ed and Joyce Gruman
Ron and Dawn Hall
Christa Kiefer
Don and Molly McAlvany
Don and Beth McDade
Bud and Dorthea McKeever
Joel, Jeremy and Sarah McKeever
Mike and Teresa McKeever
R.E. and Linda McMaster
Roger and Barb Minor
Ruth Patterson
Pat and Dede Robertson
Jim and Nancy Spillman
Harry and Sharon Stiritz
Mike and Marg Von Hahn
Steve and Dianna Walton

And to all of those who contributed financially in order to make this book possible.

INTRODUCTION

I do not like long introductions to a book, so I will keep this one brief.

Obviously the world is getting more violent. Riots are a frequent occurrence. As this book is being written, there are thirty-seven hot wars going on. Even after the Soviet Union has dissolved, in 1993, Russia is (was) building one attack submarine every thirty-three days at the cost of $1.5 billion. Thus, a military encounter with them is still not out of the question.

Fires can occur anyplace without warning and can burn down anyone's home or business.

Then there are acts of nature, such as earthquakes, tornados, hurricanes, floods and winter blizzards.

Any one of these manmade or natural disasters can strike almost anyplace on the earth at any time. Disasters strike suddenly. With a nuclear bombing, there probably would be only minutes of warning; with a tornado, perhaps an hour's warning; and with a hurricane or a flood, maybe a day's warning. But, by the time the warning comes, it is too late to start making preparations to properly meet those emergencies. You need to have prepared beforehand, so that you and your family can survive and be happy through them.

Speaking of surviving, many people have asked me if I am a "survivalist." I tell them that if, by that, they mean someone sitting at the entrance to a cave with a shotgun and a year's supply of dehydrated food and gold coins behind him, the answer is a resounding *no*. However, if someone stuck my head under water, if the question is, would I try to bring it up and survive, the answer is a definite *yes*.

Similarly, I think it is wisdom to have fire extinguishers in one's home in case of fire. If that is your definition of being a survivalist, then I am one. I also think it is wisdom to have some extra food stored in the event you get snowed in for two or three weeks and cannot get out to buy food. It would also be handy to have some food stored in case you were unemployed for a year. You would have the peace of mind to know that your family would not go hungry. Yet I am not at all the typical person that would be called a "survivalist."

A member of our Board of Directors is typical of many people, perhaps including you. A year ago he said that he thought he should start making some physical preparations for emergencies or disasters, but he didn't know where to begin. That was the seed of an idea that birthed this book.

In Chapter 1, we tell you the first thing you are to do if you are only going to make one item of preparation. If you want to do two things, Chapter 2 gives you the second item of priority to do, and so on down through the eleven chapters of the book. Thus, this book gives you a road map starting from where you are and clearly showing you where you can go in priority sequence, starting with the first step, second step, third step and so forth. As times get tougher and more violent, you may want to take some additional steps of preparation.

Many of the people who read the manuscript said that this book should be in every home in America. In fact, many people plan to use copies of it to give as Christmas presents and gifts on other occasions to help their friends and relatives.

Through the book, we do not give names and addresses of vendors where the various items mentioned can be purchased. Instead, for your convenience, we accumulate all of these in Appendix "B." In the main part of the book, we sometimes refer to Appendix "B" as (*B). In Appendix B, we give a description of the various vendors we recommend, then we have a list of products we have recommended which is oriented by chapters. Appendix B alone is worth the price of the entire book. It is such a valuable piece of information that has taken many years to pull together.

My wife, Jeani and I live on a 70-acre ranch in Oregon that is basically self-reliant. We have our own water supply for household use and irrigation and our own long-term electricity generating capacity. We have a 70-tree orchard, a 200-vine vineyard and a large garden. We raise sheep for meat and wool, goats for milk, chickens for eggs and meat, and a few turkeys for meat. We even grow lemon trees and vegetables all winter long in the greenhouse, have grown wheat and could grow everything we need here, but salt. Between Jeani and myself, we have had over forty years experience in the things discussed in this book. We have either done them or have personally researched them in depth.

We gladly pass along to you the results of our experience and any wisdom gained in these areas. Our desire is that this will help you to physically prepare for the progressively more turbulent days that lie ahead.

May God bless you,

Dr. James McKeever

PREFACE

Preparing for emergencies is one of those things that most of us would readily agree makes some sense. Yet it is easy to procrastinate and put off actually making any preparations when you are not faced with an immediate disaster. Some of the natural disasters of recent years have certainly helped to bring this need for some basic emergency readiness to the forefront of the minds of many people in this country, and that is a good thing.

As with other important things in life, there comes a time when you just need *to decide to make some time and do it.* The good news is that this book gives you an easy plan to follow. It has a veritable wealth of information, sources and resources that will literally save you many hundreds of hours, were you to try to compile all of this information on your own. With the guidelines and priority sequence provided for you here, you can simply start at the beginning and make whatever provisions you feel impressed to make and which fit within your budget. You may wish to do the first seven steps, for example, and then wait on the others.

The level of preparedness at which each family feels comfortable will differ. That's fine. The important thing is to think through these issues for *your* household and to get started *now* with whatever preparations for emergencies you feel inclined to make. Some of them are very simple and inexpensive (cost is not an excuse), but they can make an incredible difference in your comfort level immediately following a disaster.

Sometimes the woman in the home will be the one who has more time to order and organize supplies. Ideally, it can become a fun family project in which everyone participates, as outlined in Chapter 11. Only you know what division of responsibilities, time and labor makes sense for your family. But once you make it a priority to "get your house in order" in this regard, then you can relax and be at peace, knowing that you have done the best you can, given your abilities, resources and your view of the future, and you are not totally unprepared due to slothfulness or procrastination.

Good intentions are not enough; being prepared requires some time and effort. But peace of mind is one of the precious fruits you can reap, as well as acquiring some provisions that will be of use in any number of types of potential emergency situations that could occur at any time. Also, the training to your children that will be accomplished by working on this project of emergency preparedness together could prove invaluable and even someday save their lives. *The price of a small investment of your time for some amount of "emergency insurance" is well worth it!* I have no doubt that this book will be an invaluable asset to you as you examine your personal state of preparedness for emergencies.

Wishing you the best life has to offer,

Jeani McKeever

ACKNOWLEDGMENTS

First and foremost, I want to acknowledge my coauthor in this work, my lovely wife, Jeani McKeever. Not only did she write portions of it and provide many helpful suggestions and insights, but she also edited and proofread the book. She has been my inspiration and my encouragement. She is the perfect wife and co-laborer and I continually thank the Lord for her.

I also appreciate the outstanding work of Louise Hall in typing the manuscript and typesetting the book and Ellen Thorsen for her time volunteered in proofreading. In addition, I am very indebted to the men and women who went through the manuscript and gave me constructive feedback:

Jim Burck, PhD., Psychological Counseling
Maj. Lloyd Darlington, U.S. Army
Ed Gruman, Management of World Vision
Dr. Beth McDade, Retired Dentist
Roger Minor, Attorney
Mrs. Ruth Patterson, Retired Nursing Supervisor
Harry Stiritz, CPA and Tax Expert
Harry Weyandt, Nitro-Pak Preparedness Center
Col. Speed Wilson, Retired U.S. Marines

I would also like to express my appreciation of Dr. Don and Beth McDade who provided a major portion of the finances for this project and who were a real encouragement to us. Their contributions along with the contributions of those who ordered a prepublication autographed copy, have made this book possible. After you read it, I believe you will agree that we owe them all a debt of gratitude.

I also appreciate the prayers and encouragement of a whole host of people, especially the Omega Partners and our staff at Omega headquarters.

I also want to thank you for purchasing a copy of this book. My prayer and desire is that you would not only gain knowledge from this information-packed volume, but that you would then actually make the preparations you need to make.

Dr. James McKeever
P.O. Box 1788
Medford, Oregon 97501

COPUBLISHERS FELLOWSHIP

Thank You
from Jeani McKeever-Harroun

We have had a steady stream of requests for a reprint of this book since the first edition. We are very happy to be able to make it available once more, in this new, updated version, as the need for its message and tips on preparedness are more relevant than ever.

However, this printing would not have been possible without the financial support of our "Co-publishers Fellowship." Those individuals listed below have all contributed to making this reprint a reality. *A big, heartfelt thank you to each one of you!*

Beckary Systems
Gary & Liz Bowman
Susan Critelli
Donald Detrick
Kenneth & Kristen Dickerson
Roy & Josephine Dykeman

Judy Gore
Jack Harroun
Doug & Diane Kanarowski
Daniel & Sue Parnel
Lois Swanson
Dr. Mary Ruth Swope

Chapter 1

DISASTERS STRIKE SUDDENLY (WHAT IS MOST IMPORTANT?)

During 1992 we had some major catastrophes occur, as nature unleashed a tiny drop of her power. We had the Los Angeles earthquake, the tidal wave that hit Nicaragua, Hurricane Andrew in Florida, and Hurricane Iniki in Hawaii, an earthquake in Utah and a major storm in China. The loss in lives and property from those events could have been significantly greater had they been centered in highly populated areas.

In July of 1993, the flooding of the Mississippi forced thousands of families to evacuate their homes and caused much property damage and hardship in the midwest. In the same month, Japan suffered its worst earthquake in many years.

What if the epicenter of the Los Angeles earthquake had been in the middle of Los Angeles rather than up in the high desert? The death toll and property damage could have been astronomical. What if a thirty-foot tidal wave had hit the coast of California or Honolulu instead of a relatively deserted area of Nicaragua? The loss of lives and property likewise could have been astronomical. What if Hurricane Andrew had hit in the Miami-Ft. Lauderdale area rather than down on the southern tip of Florida and had gone across the gulf and hit New Orleans rather than a much less inhabited area of Louisiana? Again, the loss of lives and property would have been colossal.

Each of us need to be aware that a major catastrophe could strike any part of our country at any time. In most areas of the United States, at least one of the following could occur very suddenly:

1. A major earthquake
2. A volcanic eruption
3. A tidal wave
4. A hurricane
5. A tornado
6. A severe winter storm
7. Flooding
8. A major fire
9. Fallout from a nuclear explosion
10. Riots

One or more of these could hit your community tonight and you could be without electricity for weeks. You could be without fresh water for days and potentially without food for weeks. It is also possible that you could be without shelter, as many of the unfortunate people in Florida found themselves in the aftermath of Hurricane Andrew.

Many people are caught up with making money. This is important. However, in a time of natural or man-made catastrophes, money is of little value. Following Hurricane Andrew, in some parts of Florida, a jug of water was being sold for $30 and a bag of ice for $10! If your children were very hungry, you would be willing to pay almost any amount of money to buy food for them.

Most people do not know exactly how to prepare for emergencies in general. Many are confused about food storage; some people bought some dehydrated food back in the 70's, stored it for ten years, and then gave it away (or threw it away). Every individual needs some good, solid knowledge before he can act intelligently in this regard. This book will provide you with a lot of practical information and knowledge about how to respond in emergencies and to be prepared ahead of time for them. Knowledge is power.

There is an old saying that when you need road flares, you cannot buy any. When you need fire insurance (i.e. when your house is burning), you can't buy any. All types of emergency preparation, which essentially are in the category of insurance, need to be made ahead of time. After Hurricane Andrew hit in

Florida, it was too late for people there to try to buy food for storage or to buy an electrical generator or store up water.

This book is designed to help you be around, well, and healthy after a time of catastrophe, so that you can either enjoy the money you have earned, or use it to help others, or both. Later we will also recommend some good instructional videos that can help you with your emergency preparation and gaining knowledge in practical skills.

The information in this book could potentially even save your life. We are not prophets of doom and gloom any more than a bank that requires you to buy fire insurance on your home before they will give you a mortgage. The principals of that bank know that it is best to be prepared and protected against emergencies. We are sure you are at least as wise as your bank.

A STORM CELLAR

As a boy, I grew up in and around Dallas, Texas, which is part of the "tornado alley." I have actually seen tornadoes touch down in the Dallas area and have driven by and seen the incredible aftermath of a tornado. Some of my relatives lived on farms around Dallas and some lived in town, but just about every one of them had a storm cellar where they could go, in case a tornado was going to hit.

Consider for a moment what life might have been like if someone had had a well-supplied storm cellar in the southern tip of Florida during Hurricane Andrew or in Hawaii during Hurricane Iniki in 1992. I am sure that you can imagine that things would have been much easier for that family. They would not have had to depend on the government to bring in food and other essentials.

An interesting thought occurred to me during the aftermath of Hurricane Andrew. What if a major war had erupted someplace in the world (another Desert Storm) and all of our military and their concentrated efforts had been needed to go there instead of to southern Florida? I would rather be prepared to take care of myself, and then use anything that the government can give me as supplemental, rather than relying on the government and placing my survival and my life entirely in their hands.

HURRICANE ANDREW

By all estimates, Hurricane Andrew is by far the most costly catastrophe we have had in the United States. Estimates of the damage in southern Florida range from $7 billion to $20 billion, with an additional $1 billion worth of damage in Louisiana. The map in Figure 1.1 shows the areas of Southern Florida that were hit. As you can see, they were all south of the Miami-Ft. Lauderdale area.

As the map shows, one week after Hurricane Andrew hit, there were still 680,000 homes without electricity. So many people, at least in America, rely on electricity to light their homes, cook their meals, heat their water and run a whole host of gadgets upon which they have come to rely. If we want light, the capability of cooking, and heat without electricity, then we will need to prepare ahead of time to provide those things independent of electricity. An excellent video tape, *Preparation For Emergencies,* gives very practical things you can do in preparing to be without electricity. The address where it can be purchased is given in Appendix B. To conserve space, whenever you see (*B) in this book, that means that the address is given in Appendix B.

SEVERE WINTER OF 1992-1993

In February 1993, the entire north and eastern parts of the United States were hit by a three-week blizzard. In many parts of that region, people were without electricity and were snowed in for up to three weeks. Thus, they had to rely on whatever supplies and resources they had on hand.

There were a large number of reasons for the forecast of a severe winter for 1992-1993. Also forecast was the likelihood that the winter of 1993-1994 could likely be a very severe one.

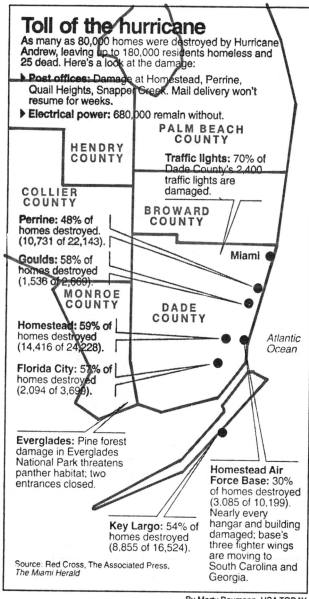

Toll of the hurricane

As many as 80,000 homes were destroyed by Hurricane Andrew, leaving up to 180,000 residents homeless and 25 dead. Here's a look at the damage:

▶ **Post offices:** Damage at Homestead, Perrine, Quail Heights, Snapper Creek. Mail delivery won't resume for weeks.

▶ **Electrical power:** 680,000 remain without.

PALM BEACH COUNTY

HENDRY COUNTY

Traffic lights: 70% of Dade County's 2,400 traffic lights are damaged.

COLLIER COUNTY

BROWARD COUNTY

Perrine: 48% of homes destroyed. (10,731 of 22,143).

Miami

Goulds: 58% of homes destroyed (1,536 of 2,669).

MONROE COUNTY

DADE COUNTY

Homestead: 59% of homes destroyed (14,416 of 24,228).

Atlantic Ocean

Florida City: 57% of homes destroyed (2,094 of 3,699).

Everglades: Pine forest damage in Everglades National Park threatens panther habitat; two entrances closed.

Homestead Air Force Base: 30% of homes destroyed (3,085 of 10,199). Nearly every hangar and building damaged; base's three fighter wings are moving to South Carolina and Georgia.

Key Largo: 54% of homes destroyed (8,855 of 16,524).

Source: Red Cross, The Associated Press. *The Miami Herald*

By Marty Baumann, USA TODAY

Figure 1.1

THE THREE TRENDS

I am a retired international consulting economist, but I am not the type of economist who depends on a crystal ball. Rather, if I can find three points on a trend, draw a straight line through them and project this line into the future, I feel that I can get a fair idea of what the future will be like in that regard, assuming that there is no tendency for that trend to reverse itself. There are many trends that I could analyze here, such as the continual rising of taxes, the oil and energy trends, the trend toward increased bureaucracy, the federal deficit trend, and so on. However, I will limit this discussion to the three outlined below.

The first trend deals with the amount of money spent in our welfare, give-away programs. In 1935, when the Social Security and Welfare system went into effect, there was 1 beneficiary for every 143 workers. Today there is 1 beneficiary for every 1.7 workers, and if you include government employees (like the 20,000 in the energy department) who economically do not produce any goods and services, it is 1 to 1. Add to this the baby boom of World War II. When all of those children hit college, we used temporary buildings and built new ones, which are now empty. About the year 2000 to 2005, these people are all going to retire *en masse*. At that point in time, we probably are going to have at least 2 or 3 beneficiaries per worker. At some point along that line, the system has to break down. The workers simply will not be able to support that many beneficiaries, and so we are coming to a crisis there.

The second trend deals with interest payments. When I was a boy, my father and my grandfather had this philosophy: Owe no man anything; if you can't pay cash, don't go. There was very little private borrowing and there was very little deficit spending. Therefore, in 1935 the interest payments were a very tiny percent of the GNP (Gross National Product), as it used to be called. Today in the U.S., interest payments on public and private debt are approximately 40-50 percent of the GDP (Gross Domestic Product). When we extrapolate that line out, and you know how compound interest goes, what happens when interest payments become 60, 70, 80, or 90 percent of the GDP? There is a breaking point at which the interest payments can no longer be supported.

The third trend is the downtrend of the U.S. dollar. You are all familiar with the price escalation that we are going through. A few years ago—say twenty years ago—bread was $.12 a loaf and either a paper dollar or a silver dollar would buy eight loaves of bread. Today bread is about $1.25 a loaf. But a silver dollar will still buy eight loaves of bread, because a silver dollar today costs about ten paper dollars. The ratio between silver and bread has not changed very much. Paper money has just become that worthless. As I extrapolate that out, I see paper money eventually becoming worth *less* and *less*.

Consequences of the Trends

All of these trends seem to be approaching a critical point somewhere between now and the year 2000. I don't know when the exact breakdown is going to be. I don't think that anyone does. But let us consider what will happen when things do break down. What is likely to happen in real terms when the workers can no longer support the beneficiaries? I believe that at some point the government is going to have to decide to freeze the payments that they are giving to the beneficiaries, in spite of the fact that prices will be continually increasing. If that is done, I think that it will only last for a few months. The time will come when the check that the welfare recipients get from the government will barely buy their rent and food. Soon afterward it will only pay their rent, but it will not buy their food. Then what happens? For three generations, the do-gooders have been telling the freeloaders that they have a right to be supported. When their check will not buy the things that they think they have a right to, I believe that they will simply go in and take those things from the stores.

What happens when the interest payments become unbearable? Governments, in all past history, who have encountered this problem have normally repudiated the debt. This means that all bonds, among other things, would be cancelled, because the interest payments would break the back of the economy. Four-fifths of the volume of Wall Street is bonds, and only one-fifth is stocks. If bonds were all cancelled, Wall Street would be out of business. Were that to happen, either the U.S. government would subsidize it or come in and actually run it.

What happens when the paper money becomes worthless? It is likely that people would just stop going to work. Who is going to want to work for worthless paper? If the firemen, the telephone company employees, utility company employees, gas station operators, and mailmen all stopped going to work, we would have a breakdown of services.

I believe that many of the forces have been set into motion that will cause an economic crisis of gigantic proportions sometime between now and the year 2000.

There are many other things that could create a crisis, such as an oil embargo, substantially higher oil prices, or a military confrontation with Russia (even though the Soviet Union has disbanded) or with some other country. If one of these other crises does not get us, the economic one will.

WHEN WILL IT HAPPEN?

I have spoken at major economic and monetary conferences around the world, where I have had innumerable people ask me, "How much time do we have?" My reply is always, "How much time do we have to do what?" Whatever their answer is, I tell them to simply go and do it *now*. I would rather be ten years too early than ten minutes too late in any kind of preparation.

Sometimes at conferences, people come up and ask me, "When do you think we are going to have the big crash and what should I do?" I ask them to define for me what they mean by, "the big crash." Generally they really cannot do so. My reply is to tell them that if they are talking about bank failures, they should put their money in one of the top ten banks in the United States, because the U.S. government has already proven, when the Continental Illinois Bank in Chicago was about to go under, that they would not let any major bank go under.

Therefore, if their concern is about banks, it would be advisable to put their money into one of the largest banks. If they are concerned about a stock market crash, I tell them simply to take their money out of the stock market. I further tell them that if they are concerned about a depression, the kind where prices are falling, they can simply move their assets into cash and wait for the drop to be completed, at which time they could go in and buy things perhaps at 10 cents on the dollar.

I find that there is a great deal of fear among people concerning an ominous giant "black cloud" they call "The Crash." Yet if they stop to analyze exactly what is it that they really need to prepare for, then the answers become relatively simple.

I or any other thinking person can come up with multiple possible scenarios of the future. These can range from Russia making a nuclear attack on the United States (which is still possible) to the United States and Russia being united against China. They can range from a belief that we have hit the bottom of our fifty-year cycle and we are about to start the next upward boom, to believing that we are just about to start the major down leg of our fifty-year cycle.

There is a wide variety of human forecasts of the future that can be of interest and can give us helpful input in coming up with our own view of the future. Your view of the future is what you will live by and I think it is important to give attention to the potentiality of emergencies or disasters happening in your area and how they might affect you and your family.

The fact is that many factors from different directions point to the likelihood that you could experience some sort of disaster within your lifetime. If you give any credence to the Bible at all, it is interesting to note that the Bible also forecasts some troubled times ahead, both geologically and in other ways. For a detailed discussion of what the Scriptures have to say and project, I refer you to a book I have written entitled *The Future Revealed* (*B). It may be of interest to you to note that the Bible specifically forecasts a coming major war, famines, earth upheavals, the persecution of Christians, lawlessness increasing and other cataclysmic events. These are all forecast to occur *before* what the Bible calls the great tribulation. If you are one of the Christians who believe that we are likely living at the end of this age, you would be wise to prepare for these disasters that are predicted.

Because of my Judeo-Christian heritage, I (like multiplied millions around the world) see the Bible as an enduring book full of wisdom. Consequently, in this work I will occasionally quote from it, when it sheds light on a particular subject. I trust that this does not offend you. But if it does, perhaps the valuable information in this book will enable you to overlook these references. I am all for wisdom, wherever it is found.

THE FOUR AREAS OF PREPARATION

We have seen that disasters can strike suddenly. The earthquakes in San Francisco and Los Angeles area came without warning and one never knows when we will have another severe winter, like the one in 1992-1993, or worse. Floods, earthquakes, tornadoes, fires and other such disasters can occur unexpectedly. The time to prepare for such things is *now*, ahead of time.

We discussed three trends which I have observed in my work as an economist. Without some major economic turn-around, which does not appear likely, these trends are going to grind on regardless of who is in the White House. The interest payments will continue to compound. In fact, Peter Grace and the Grace Commission reported to the President of the United States that they estimated that by the year 2000 our federal debt would be $9.7 trillion. My own estimate is that it will be over $12 trillion. The interest on that magnitude of debt is going to eat us alive. The baby boomers are going to retire and they are going to need to be supported, and the U.S. dollar continues to get weaker and weaker. Today, it is worth 25 cents compared to a 1970 dollar.

In looking at these events—the natural and man-made disasters as well as the events the Bible forecasts that will occur at the end of this age—there are four areas of preparation that would be wise to consider. If you believe as I do that these events could likely come and that you may experience them, here are the four areas of possible preparation for your consideration:

1. Spiritual preparation
2. Physical preparation
3. Financial preparation
4. Social (freedom) preparation

To me, the spiritual preparation is by far the most important. I would hate to survive physically and financially and come through it all bitter, angry at the world, disillusioned and sour. I pity the man who finds himself in that state. I believe we need to have peace with our Creator.

Of course, physical survival is very important. The other considerations are unimportant if we are not physically alive. This is basic.

Yet you could survive major crises physically but be destitute, like many of the refugees all over the world. Therefore, financial preparation is also very important.

The last area of social preparation or preparation in regard to freedom and community, is also very important. I would hate to survive physically and financially and wind up under a horrible dictatorship. This is not a very pleasant prospect.

There are forthcoming books in this Preparation Series on these other three areas. Physical preparation for emergencies or disasters is the area that this book primarily addresses. First let us discuss what I consider to be the most important aspect of physical preparation.

IMMEDIATELY AFTER A DISASTER

In the first part of this chapter, we discussed various natural or man-made disasters or catastrophes that could occur suddenly. The first 72 hours following a disaster are very critical. You may need to leave your home, or the authorities may force you to evacuate your home. Also, you may not be at home when a disaster occurs. For example, people have been caught up in the mountains in their automobile in a severe snowstorm and have been snowed in for two or three days. Alternatively, you could be out traveling on a vacation when a major disaster strikes. So, let's specifically consider the first two or three days immediately following a disaster that could be very critical to you and your family.

If you are fortunate, you may be at home. However, it is just as likely that you could be at work, on a trip, on vacation, at some friends' place or elsewhere when an unexpected emergency or natural disaster strikes. During those initial hours or days, you may not have access to any long-term supplies that you may have stored at home, at least until you are able to get home. That may even be on foot, if roadways are damaged or blocked, such as following a major earthquake.

Therefore, having some form of portable emergency supplies in a container in your vehicle would be recommended. Some companies carry what they call "72-hour kits" which include critical items that you would be likely to need in those first three days, wherever you might be. Or you could create you own. Keep in mind things such as:

1. Water
2. A small first aid kit
3. Ready-to-eat foods
4. A space blanket (folds into a very small space but holds in heat extremely efficiently)

A homemade kit including basic supplies can be assembled very inexpensively for about $15-$20, including the items listed above. Granola bars and other high energy, ready-to-eat foods are recommended, since water could be limited. (High protein foods require a lot of water to digest.)

Companies carrying three- and seven-day emergency preparedness systems of various types (a five-year shelf life on water and foods) are listed in Appendix B (*B). As of 1993, a 72-hour kit including food, water and other supplies could be purchased for as little as $20 plus freight.

Some of these kits contain "no cook" meals, such as the excellent ones made by Alpine Aire. But to these you still must add water. For hot dishes, you should add hot water. Finding and heating water may present a problem immediately following a disaster, so you should also consider "Meals Ready To Eat" which require no addition of water.

Military MRE's (Meals Ready To Eat)

Military MRE's (which stand for "Meals Ready to Eat") are worth consideration particularly for the first two or three days of immediate emergency following a disaster or crisis. MRE's are available commercially, and they come in a wide variety of meal choices such as Beef Stew, Tuna and Noodles, Chicken à la King, Spaghetti with Meat Sauce, Chicken and Rice, and so forth.   During a time when you may be in transition or trying to relocate to where your long-term supplies are stored, these can provide instant meals without worry or fuss about cooking or heating. They are just that–ready to eat. They are an are excellent transitional food, providing full, complete meals. They come in extremely strong boxes that contain 12 complete meal packets. That is a three-day supply for a family of four eating two meals a day of 1500-1800 calories per meal.

Each MRE package also has in it a packet which contains: toilet tissue, matches, a moist towelette, salt and the makings for coffee. However, with the MRE, you would still need a beverage or water to drink or with which to make coffee. You do not need to add water to the MRE itself, as you do with the "no cook meals."

These MRE's are also great for emergency evacuation, if you needed to leave a place quickly. You could literally grab a case and go. They are fast and easy. You can eat them cold or warm them up if you have means to do so. You can boil the pouch in water, even in dirty water, since it is completely sealed, or you could even lay them in the sun to warm them. Shelf-life at normal temperatures (70 degrees), is eight years. The MRE's are a great transitional supply for the 72-hour immediate need after an emergency, while you begin to use your longer-term food storage.

SUMMARY AND CONCLUSION

All of the forms of preparation suggested in this book are just different forms of insurance. Like fire insurance, you hope that you never have to use it, but you have it if you need it. It is really an investment that could potentially pay off some big dividends.

We have seen that there are many trends that could possibly lead to economic disasters, riots, looting and even military disasters. There are many natural disasters that could strike suddenly in any part of the country. We also noted that the Bible forecast certain catastrophes would occur in days to come, which included war, famine, earth upheavals and an increase in lawlessness.

STEP 1: PURCHASE A 72-HOUR SURVIVAL KIT FOR EACH MEMBER OF YOUR FAMILY.

The probability for catastrophes occurring is rapidly increasing, in my opinion. Therefore, if you would like to make some longer-term preparations for emergencies and disasters, after you have made preparations to survive the first 72 hours, what is the first and most important thing that you should do to prepare? We will discuss this in the next chapter.

We will deal with relevant concerns in their order of importance. Therefore, you can make the preparations outlined in Chapters 1 and 2 and stop there, or you can make preparations based on the recommendations of the first three chapters and stop there. You can go as far with preparations as you would like to go or feel impressed to go. I am going to give them to you in what I feel is the order of importance. So let us move on to the next most important consideration, after you have made some provision for the first 72 hours after a crisis.

Chapter 2

WATER, WATER, WATER

As noted in Chapter 1, natural and man-made disasters occur with great regularity, including:

Hurricanes	Tornadoes
Flooding	Earthquakes
Tidal waves	Volcanic eruptions
Riots	Fires
Snow storms	Terrorism

One or more of these disasters could strike your area suddenly, at almost any time. In almost any of these, there is a good possibility that you could be without water service, gas service and electricity for days or even weeks.

In order to consider what you might want to do in the physical realm to prepare for these potential crises, in this chapter, we will continue with the *second* most important item of preparation and then work down the list from there in each subsequent chapter. After you have read this entire book, you can then decide how far you want to go in your personal or your family's preparation. It may be the suggestions outlined in just Chapters 1 and 2, or it might be Chapters 1 through 7, or it may be the entire list of things. This gives you a priority sequence and a place to start.

The number one consideration for survival beyond the initial three days, and by far the most important, is to have access to drinkable water. A man can go thirty or forty days or even more without food, but he can only go maximum of three or four days without water or he will die. In Florida, immediately after Hurricane Andrew in 1992, in some places, water was selling for as much as $30 per jug of water. A natural disaster could hit almost any part of the country at any time. In the vast majority of these, the first and most important need is for fresh drinking water.

In July of 1993, following the severe flooding of the Mississippi, newsmen reported 300,000 people in the Des Moines, Iowa area alone were without drinking water, and they were looking at seven to thirty days before they would have water again! That is incredible, and yet such crises can occur without warning. We think of flooding as being an *excess* of water, which indeed it is, in areas where we don't want water. The reason that people were without drinking water was because purification plants were flooded with contaminated sewage from damaged sewer systems. Although there was water everywhere, there was none to drink! People were standing in lines to get a jug of water. If they had had their own purifier or some water stored, they could have had their own source of drinking water during this catastrophe.

Water is an inexpensive and easy thing to store when it is available. It is something of tremendous value when you don't have any.

There are basically three ways that you can ensure that you will have a source of drinkable water:

1. Store water
2. Be able to purify water (and have a source)
3. Have a deep, personally-controlled well

Of the three alternatives, by far the best one for most people who live in urban or very dry areas is the storage of water. Obviously, most urban dwellers do not have a personally-controlled, deep well and purifying water is only a partial solution (since it may not take out some of the things that could cause damage to your body). So let's look at that consideration of storing water.

THE STORAGE OF WATER

If you are going to store water, you need to decide for what period of time will you need to rely on that stored water. It takes at least 1 gallon of water per day per person for cooking, drinking and washing your hands up to the first knuckle. To store the absolute minimum amount of water for a family of four for two weeks would require 56 gallons. However, a more realistic amount is 2 gallons of water per day per family member. For fourteen days, this would be 28 gallons per person. If you use 30- or 55-gallon water barrels, it is best to allow one barrel per person. You simply cannot store too much water. In Appendix B, you will find addresses of sources for barrels.

The next consideration is *how* to store the water. The good thing about water is that it will store for long periods of time if proper preparation is made. Enough fresh chlorine (or iodine) must be added to make sure that there is no bacterial or fungal growth. The only thing that happens to prepared water after long periods of storage is that the air separates out and the water tastes flat. This is corrected by aerating the water, which can be accomplished by pouring it from container to container, by shaking it, or by mixing it vigorously.

If money is no object, you can build your supply rapidly and without much fuss by buying enough 5-gallon containers of bottled drinking water. In checking with the drinking water suppliers, I learned that there can be fungal growth if their water is exposed to sunlight for extended periods. Therefore, each container should be placed in a heavy-duty black plastic trash sack and stored in a cool dark place. These bottles should be dated and rotated.

One thing to remember if you use glass containers is never to stack them tightly together or on shelves. In case of an earthquake or explosion, they might fall or be knocked together. For this reason, I do *not* recommend glass containers for emergency water storage.

Another way to store your water is to put it in fairly airtight plastic containers. These could be anything from used two-liter pop bottles with tight-fitting lids to large 55-gallon food-grade plastic containers. I recommend using only new food-grade containers. Old, used plastic barrels can never be fully cleaned. Don't try to cut corners with this crucial water storage.

Whatever size you choose, be sure that the containers are clean and then fill them with ordinary tap water. Add enough *fresh* bleach to make a ratio of 1 teaspoon of bleach for each 5 gallons of water in the container. This is about twice the amount recommended by some books, but I have found that it has stopped all fungal growth for over ten years. I would rather be safe than sorry when it comes to my water supply. To be safe, recheck your water supply every six months, or at least annually. After you open the container, you should be able to smell an odor of chlorine. If you do not, then replace and retreat the water.

One very easy method that some have recommended in times past as a minimal storage effort is to save any bleach bottle that you empty and fill it with tap water. I do *not* recommend this, because they are not food-grade containers and could leach toxic chemicals into the water.

Be sure not to store your water reserves by rotten potatoes, near gasoline or on a cement floor, because the water could taste like whatever it is stored upon or beside.

A better homespun solution than empty bleach bottles is the two-liter soda pop bottles. They are designed not to let odors and taste come in through the walls. You would need to add eight drops of chlorine (bleach) to the tap water to ensure that no algae growth would occur. Remember, it would take about two of these bottles per person per day, which means that it would take fourteen for each person for a week. These are quite sturdy containers and one expert has estimated that the container costs more than the liquid inside, so you might as well take advantage of these free, good "water" containers, if you or someone you know regularly consumes soda pop.

If you decide to use bottles that have been previously used for something else, or even brand new containers, it is *very important* that you sterilize them before filling them with your storage water. Of course, the first thing that you are going to want to do is to wash them thoroughly, inside and out, being sure to rinse all of the soapy water out of the inside of the bottles. Then make up a solution that consists of 1 quart water and 1/4 cup of Clorox or other liquid bleach. Fill your container with the sterilizing solution and put the cap on. You need to let this solution stand in the bottle about three minutes. (Don't forget to turn it upside down two or three times to sterilize the inside of the cap as well.) Pour the same sterilizing solution into bottle after bottle. After you have purified a bottle, you can add tap water and then add four drops of chlorine per quart (this would be 16 drops per gallon or 1 teaspoon for a 5-gallon bottle).

If you have enough space in your garage, there are companies that make 15, 20, 30 and 55-gallon FDA-approved, food-grade barrels that are designed for holding liquids for human consumption. These will not leak toxicity into the water or cooking oil or other substances that you may choose to store in the barrels. These containers are extremely heavy duty and will provide the best protection for your water reserves. One supplier reports that your house could collapse down on one of these containers without damaging it. Companies that distribute these come and go, so we will include the addresses of the companies we recommend in Appendix B. As companies change, we will update Appendix B, which is also indicated by (*B) in this book.

Another very nice and safe way to store water is in a 5-gallon, triple-lined, foil-barrier bag that is designed for water storage. These can be used over and over again. The bag fits into a box that has two handles. These boxes can be stacked up for convenience in storing. A stack of ten of these would take care of a family of four for almost two weeks. A supply source for these "water storage boxes" can be found in Appendix B.

There are many other ways to store water. I heard of one person who got some 1 x 12 lumber, built frames in his basement and had water stored in three waterbed mattresses. This is *not* recommended, since the plastic could release toxic chemicals into the water.

Also, every home has some amount of water stored, whether or not the residents realize it. There is some water stored in the water heater and in the toilet tank(s). *If an emergency came, such as an earthquake that broke all the water mains, the first thing you would want to do is to go out and shut off the water where it enters the house (or leaves the street), so that none of the water in your house would backflow out into a broken water main and no contaminated water from the water main would come into your home.*

You should also turn off the gas to your hot water heater to make sure that it does not overheat as the water supply goes down and to keep the water from becoming cloudy. Then you can safely draw water from the tank's drain valve. You may need to open a faucet somewhere in the house to provide a vent which would allow a good flow of water. If you have a two-story home, this should be an upstairs faucet. If you have a 50-gallon hot water heater, it would provide water for a family of four for about thirteen days. Be sure you know how to use the drain valve and have containers small enough to fit under it, because the valve is usually quite low to the floor. If you are going to rely on toilet tanks, you might want to scrub them out occasionally and refrain from using the dissolvable bowl cleaners and deodorizers that are made for use in the holding tank.

PURIFYING WATER

In the preceding section where we are talking about storage of water, we were assuming that you have drinkable tap water available to you. If you do not, then you are going to have to purify your own water. Also, it is possible that after your storage water runs out, you will then have to purify water to ensure its safety. *Thus, purifying water is a very important second consideration, after water storage.*

My wife and I have traveled through almost every part of the world and we have a little purifying system that we take with us. All you need is a very small bottle of this solution and two 1-quart bottles with screw-on caps. Many similar systems are found in backpacking stores and they are readily available for travel. The one we like the best is Polar Pure Iodine Crystals. One bottle treats up to 2,000 quarts of water. We use this to purify drinking water in foreign countries when needed, as we travel.

If you were in more primitive conditions or conditions with radioactive fallout, you would need to filter or strain the water first before purifying it. Let's take an extreme example. You would first strain your water through a piece of fine cloth to remove the large particles, and then strain it through a paper towel to remove many of the finer particles. It would be after this initial filtering process that you would want to use this iodine solution water disinfectant that we use. The nice thing about it is that the water is drinkable after just one hour. Another good alternative is the germicidal tablets, Potable Aqua.

You have to double check any water purifier you buy to see what is does and does not purify against. For example, some purifiers will kill all bacteria and viruses but will leave heavy metals, such as arsenic, in the water. Some of them will not filter out the microscopic particles of radioactive fallout. You want to be sure to get the filter that matches your needs.

We highly recommend the PUR Explorer (*B), a major advancement in outdoor water purification. Due to a unique, patented design, it resists clogging better than any other purifier on the market and it is the only product tested and proven to remove all microorganisms, including Giardia, viruses and bacteria. Its easy pumping action produces more than 1 liter of water per minute. Because it is lightweight and affordable, it is ideal for backpackers, campers and other outdoor enthusiasts. Ordinary water purifiers are easily clogged by leaves and sediment. The new Explorer uses a unique, circular intake filter that resists clogging, whether it is suspended in water or lying on the bottom of a lake or pond.

Ordinary purifiers must be disassembled, cleaned, then put back together. With the PUR Explorer, a simple, quarter-twist of the pump handle is all it takes to switch to the cleaning mode. A built-in brush quickly cleans the filter as you pump. Total cleaning time is measured in seconds instead of minutes or hours. The PUR Traveler is a less expensive non-pump version of the PUR Explorer.

The PUR Survivor (*B) will desalinate sea water, purify brackish or contaminated fresh water and produce great-tasting, clean fresh water.

Two other excellent filters are the Accufilter 5, a five-stage filter available as a canteen insert, straw or sport bottle, and the Swiss Katadyn Ceramic Pocket Filters which are internationally recognized as superior filters. The Katadyn filters are also the cheapest in the long run. Conservatively speaking, they will purify 5,000 gallons. There are some cheaper ones on the market, but they will only purify 500-800 gallons. They will also totally remove fallout down to .2 microns. These filters have been around for about eighty years, so we know that they are reputable.

However, it does no good whatsoever to have a water filtering system unless you have a water supply. And this takes us back to water storage. Some people may think of using their swimming pools as a source of water to be purified. This might be a viable option in some situations. However, in a nuclear fallout situation or one in which a storm blew in large amounts of dust, with all of the radioactive or dust particles falling into the pool, you would have to be sure that they were all filtered out. If there were an extreme emergency and you had made no preparation, you could always use something like a paper towel to filter the water, but obviously this is crude and it does not take everything out of the water that you would like to have taken out. Something like this should only be used in a case of last resort.

WATER ON COUNTRY PROPERTY

If some people want to buy some acreage a fairly good distance from a city as a place where they could go in emergencies, I would tell them that the three most important things to look for on that property are:

1. Water
2. WATER
3. **WATER**

There may even be a creek, stream, or river running through your property, but you need to be sure that you have water rights so you may use all that you need of that water.

A spring up the hill is ideal. That way, the water can come down by gravity and, if the spring is covered, you would not have radioactive particles falling into it, in the case of a nuclear fallout situation. However, if it were to rain and the rain began to soak those radioactive particles downward to the water table, then the spring could become contaminated.

Also, on rural property, as a viable alternative, you would like to have a deep well that you control on your own property. The reason that I emphasize deep is because it would take a long time for surface contamination to reach the water table, say 400 or 500 feet down. In addition, by the time it has gone through that much sand filtration, much of the contaminant has probably been filtered out by nature.

One disadvantage with a deep well is that you would need electricity to run the pump. If you are purely relying on the public utilities for this electricity, you are in somewhat of a compromised position. Thus, one alternative would be to have a generator that would be able to run your well. The other alternative is to have a hand pump that could be operated manually.

SUMMARY AND CONCLUSION

In the event of a nuclear disaster, you would need to be inside a fallout shelter for seven to fourteen days before it would be safe to go outside. For this, you would want to prepare to have enough drinkable water supply for a minimum of fourteen days. One of the better ways to assure yourself of having this is to have the water stored in containers in your basement, garage, or barn.

It would also be advisable to have some type of purifying system in the event that you needed to drink water from streams, lakes, or a swimming pool, so you could do the best possible job of having it purified before it goes into your body. If you were to drink water containing radioactive particles, this would be the most deadly type of exposure of all, because these particles would then be inside you and you would be hit by alpha, beta, and gamma rays—all three—continually. Drinking water contaminated with radioactive particles would be one of the surest ways to ensure your death after a nuclear incident.

If you move from an urban area to a rural area or have an alternative place to live in a rural area, then you have more options. Possibly you could get your water from a spring. In most areas, a deep well is also a viable alternative.   You usually would have more space to store water.   But remember, there are three most important things that you should consider when looking for country property.   Do you remember what those three things are?

As I said earlier, during August of 1992, when Hurricane Andrew hit the southern tip of Florida and a portion of Louisiana, in some places water was selling for as much as $30 a jug.   Some communities were without water for many days and some for as long as two months.   Then in September of 1992, Hurricane Iniki hit the northernmost of the Hawaiian Islands, the island of Kauai.   There, too, in some cases, it was two weeks before water was available.   By far and above the most important thing in these disasters, or other possible ones (next to a 72-hour kit discussed in Chapter 1), is to have some water stored and then a way to get additional pure drinking water, either by purification or by having one's own well.

In summary form then, Step 2 is this:

STEP 2:   STORE WATER AND BE ABLE TO PURIFY WATER.

Now that we have covered the second most important thing in physical preparation, let's move on to discuss the third most important item.   This would be something you would want to do *after* you have taken care of your water storage and purification needs.

Chapter 3

LET THERE BE LIGHT
(AND HEAT)

It could be somewhat debatable as to what is next in priority of physical preparation. Of course, if you do not have shelter, that would probably be a prime consideration. But in many (perhaps most) physical disasters, there will be someplace for shelter from the elements, whether it be a cave, a tent, the basement of an office building or a portion of your home or garage left standing. Of course, a more ideal situation would be having a permanent underground or basement shelter that could be used to protect you even from nuclear fallout, which could also be used as a storm shelter or as a cool place for storing root vegetables and other foods. We will address the consideration of shelter in a later chapter.

For now, let us assume that there is some type of shelter left for you after the occurrence of an emergency. Let us also assume that you made provisions so that you have an adequate water supply for your family. The question then is, what is the next (third) important preparation for you to make?

LET THERE BE LIGHT

It is possible that some kind of provision for light could be even more important than the storage of water, at least in the first few hours after a disaster. Many disasters happen at night and usually all of the electrical power goes out. Let us just say that an earthquake, a hurricane, a tornado or some other disaster occurred in the middle of the night which caused part of your roof to cave in and debris was lying everywhere with nails sticking up and broken glass all around. Suppose this disaster also caused all of the electrical power to go out. What is the first thing that you would need?

The first thing you would do well to have would be a good, working, long-lasting flashlight in or on your bedside table, so that you could see your way to step over the debris, the possible nails or broken glass in the rubble, to check on your children or to find an appropriate exit from your home.

Most people have never experienced true darkness, unless they have been inside the Carlsbad Caverns, the Oregon Caves, or similar situations where the lights were turned off and there were no secondary sources providing partial light, such as the moon or stars. If you have been to one of these places, you know that you can hold your hand one inch in front of your eyes and you cannot even see your hand. In most communities, there is so much sky light from reflection from the atmosphere and various other places that we really do not experience true darkness in our homes. However, in the situation described above, you are likely to experience true blackness and you will need some type of light.

In addition to a flashlight, there are the little safety lights that you can plug into your wall sockets that stay continually charged from your regular household current and come on when the electricity goes off. These, too, can be used as very short-lived flashlights. These are nice in that they are very handy, and we have some ourselves, but they do not take the place of a good, powerful, flashlight to keep near your bedside.

Immediately after a disaster, *do not* flip on a light switch or use a candle, kerosene lamp or a Coleman lantern. The reason for this is that there could be a broken gas pipe and gas could be escaping. One little lit match or spark from a light switch is all that it would take for the entire place to go up.

In fact, one of the first things you would want to do after the emergency would be to get to the main gas valve in your house and shut it off. Make sure you have an adjustable wrench or gas shut off tool stored near your gas meter. And as we have said, you should also shut off the main water feed to your house, so that the water in your home will not drain backward or any contaminated water in the water main will not contaminate the water in your home. One of our recommended vendors (*B) offers a combination gas and water shut off multitool, called "On-Duty" that is made specifically for this purpose.

In this first portion of our discussion on providing light, we are just looking at the emergency light needed immediately after a disaster occurs. Not only is it good to have one flashlight by your bedstand, but somewhere in a handy place, there should be at least one good flashlight for every person in your home. To ensure that you have this, I recommend that you actually place the name of the person on the flashlight, either with an engraver or on a little piece of paper attached securely with scotch tape. Every individual needs his own source of light and needs to know where it is kept and be responsible for checking it periodically to be sure the batteries have not run down.

There are other things that you may want to do immediately after an emergency. First, you would want to put out any fires that may have been started. (Fire extinguishers are discussed in Chapter 5.) Second, you would want to give first aid to anyone hurt in the emergency. We will leave discussion of those two subjects for the next two chapters and continue here with the subject of light.

WHAT HAPPENS AFTER SUNSET?

Try to imagine a situation in which your house has been destroyed, but you and your family are able to set up camping in your garage, which miraculously was left standing. You have water stored and all day long you are out working, cleaning away the debris and sawing off the trees that have fallen across your driveway. As the sun begins to set, and it begins to darken, you get back together and hopefully eat (we will talk about food in a subsequent chapter). It now goes totally dark, since no electricity has even begun to be restored in your neighborhood. The question then arises, what do you do all evening in the dark? Very likely you would find it extremely unnerving to be without any light. In fact, darkness was one of the plagues that God brought upon Egypt as the children of Israel were exiting. Even the cowboys in the western movies had a campfire to give them warmth, but it primarily gave them *light.*

One way or the other, you are going to need to provide some light so that you can read, play games, do hobbies, or whatever type of evening activity that might seem desirable to you. But every one of these activities requires some light. Thus, you need to make preparation to provide some type of ongoing light for the evenings (and possibly early mornings). Flashlights are not that adequate on a long-term, ongoing basis, because eventually their batteries run down. You may want to store extra batteries. After Hurricane Andrew and the San Francisco earthquake, the stores were almost instantly sold out of batteries. They were being sold on the street for five times their regular prices. If you place extra batteries in your freezer, the shelf life is almost indefinite. (You may wish to store some extra flashlight bulbs, as well.)

Rechargeable batteries will not do you any good, because there may not be any electricity with which to recharge them. There are solar-powered battery rechargers available that would be a possibility for rechargeable batteries (*B).

One of the most desirable ways to provide ongoing light would be to have a small, electrical generator that would be gasoline or propane powered. You can find these in Ace Hardware stores, at Sears or other stores. They are lightweight and can be carried by hand or rolled like a wheelbarrow. I would recommend a generator that produces at least 1500 watts. You would need an extension cord and some electric lamps that could be plugged into it. This electrical generator could also be used during the daytime for brief periods to run a skill saw, a wheat grinder, and other helpful appliances. A small diesel generator would be even more desirable, but I have never seen or heard of one.

I once lived out in an isolated cove on Catalina Island, where we had no electricity. But we did have a small generator, which I used in a very unusual, but efficient way. I was building a cabin, so all morning I would measure the lumber and mark it where I needed to make saw cuts and where I needed to drill holes. Right after lunch, I would fire up the generator for about thirty minutes and do all of my cutting and drilling at once. Then I would shut off the generator, and all afternoon I would nail up the lumber that I had cut during my "thirty minute power break." So a small electrical generator could not only give you light, but it could be very helpful and an excellent resource in other ways as well. However, purchasing a generator would be a lower priority than buying the things mentioned in the next two chapters.

LIGHT BY FLAME

Once you are absolutely sure that there is no gas in the area, you could use candles, kerosene lamps, or Coleman lanterns for light. You can get 100-hour candles from some of the companies mentioned in Appendix B. These are nice but, as with any candle, they do give off some soot.

Kerosene lamps, such as the Aladdin lamp (* B), can be very nice and give a bright light and they do not give a sooty discharge. The kerosene Aladdin lamps have a gauze-type mantle similar to a Coleman lantern, that works in conjunction with a full circle wick to produce a bright light, which is the equivalent of a 60-watt bulb. These lanterns are much brighter than the regular, wick only, kerosene lamps.

There are excellent Coleman lanterns available. This is the type with the two mantels (which remind me of doll socks). These are either run by gasoline or propane. I highly recommend the propane variety. Of course, you would need to store some bottles of propane. These propane bottles would not only be handy for lighting the Coleman lanterns, but possibly also for cooking. (Don't be impatient—I told you we would discuss food later.)

Of course, you could do as the cowboys did and have a bonfire, but a campfire is a crude source of light. Even back in the Biblical days, they had oil lamps. But, by whatever method you may choose, lighting with a flame is a viable method of long-term light provision.

CHEMICAL LIGHT

There is a unique source of light which is chemical in nature and does not us a flame nor electricity, and it produces no heat. These lights, called "Snaplights," come in a plastic tube about 8 inches long and are available in various colors. Inside the tube is a glass vial with a separate chemical. You bend the plastic tube, which breaks the glass inside; then you shake it to produce light. The eight-hour and twelve-hour ones produce light that is bright enough that you can read by it, if you hold it over the page. People have even used these chemical lights to light a party. The thirty-minute variety is four times brighter than the eight or twelve hour ones. There is also an orange five-minute chemical light that is fifty times brighter then the regular ones. All of these are safe to use even when gas might be present. Again, guess where you can find the address of where to buy these chemical lights?...You've got it—Appendix B.

HEAT FOR WARMTH AND COOKING

The reason we are including heat with light is that almost all of the sources that create light also generate heat, except fluorescent lights and chemical lights. All the other forms of light that burn something, such as oil lamps, kerosene lamps, gas or propane lamps create heat in the burning process. All tungsten bulbs generate heat, as you know if you have ever tried to unscrew a light bulb with your bare hands that has been on for sometime. In fact, people use electric lights as the heat source in chick brooders. We are not talking about heat lights; we are talking about regular, white light bulbs.

The need for heat for warmth will depend a great deal on geography. If it is summer or you live in the South or in the tropics, heat is not a real need. If you are living in the San Diego area or the southern Florida area, you could probably get by comfortably without any extra heat for warmth. In fact, sometimes heat is an undesirable addition. In earlier days, the ladies in the South did their canning on a wood stove placed outside, so that they did not heat up the house.

However, if you live in a cooler climate, and especially if a disaster occurred in the winter, providing heat, especially at night, would be highly desirable. A wood stove is a very good option. Fireplaces are inefficient and not a good choice of a heat source. If you have a fireplace, a fireplace insert would be recommended. A fireplace insert looks like, and essentially is, a wood stove, but it is designed to have its smoke go up the fireplace chimney instead of up a stovepipe.

There are small, portable propane heaters and kerosene heaters which are designed for space heating that are excellent (*B). You would need to purchase these ahead of time, learn to use them and have ample fuel on hand. It may be wise to store not only the small 16-ounce size, but also the larger 5-gallon size, which can be refilled. There is an adaptor available so that these larger tanks can be used with both lanterns and heaters.

Incidentally, these small propane heaters can have many uses. You can take one with you when you ice skate on a frozen pond. You can take one with you when you are working outside in the biting cold. I have even used one to thaw out frozen pipes. It is nice to have some handy, portable heat for many reasons.

Of course, you should use the type that matches the type of fuel that you have stored. It is possible in many rural places, and sometimes even in the city, to have a 1000-gallon propane tank which could be used very adequately to provide warmth.

If at all possible, I recommend having a 55-gallon drum of kerosene with a hand pump on it and some kerosene heating or cooking devices.

In many ways, propane is preferable over kerosene, because it burns cleaner and does not smell. The choice is one of both economics and convenience.

You do need to be able to cook food in most emergencies, and so some type of camp stove that is kerosene-or propane-powered would make life easier. Using charcoal for heat or cooking indoors in dangerous because of the carbon monoxide emissions. Charcoal fires should only be used outside where there is adequate ventilation. The most desirable cooking would be electric, since there would not be any danger of explosion from gases that may be in your area or may come into your area.

You should check with your local fire department for any fuel storage restrictions. Also check with your insurance company to be sure the fuel storage does not invalidate your fire insurance or homeowner's policy.

A MOTOR HOME

If you have enough money to own a motor home, you will already have many of the things discussed in Chapters 2 and 3. A motor home usually has water storage (although limited), a generator, lights, heat and limited fuel storage. But it does *not* have the things addressed in the other chapters, including Chapter 1. But if you can afford it, a motor home is a good investment for disaster preparation.

SUMMARY AND CONCLUSION

In so many emergencies, the electricity in the entire community goes off. If the emergency occurs at night, you will need an immediate, close-at-hand source of light to help you exit a building, check on loved ones, turn off the gas and water and other immediate needs.

If the results of the disaster last for many days, you will need a way to provide light for yourself in the evenings. Probably, the most ideal way to do this is with a small electrical generator that could not only provide light, but possibly run a small radio or television set.

Another age-old alternative for providing light in the evening is with a flame. We discussed candles, kerosene lamps and Coleman propane lanterns. There is even chemical light, which is nice and certainly would have advantages if there were gas in the area, but these are not all that practical for long-term use, since they only can be used once.

In a time of emergency, if your electricity were out for an extended period, you would need light in order to read, play games, do hobbies and other types of things during the evenings. Providing light would be our third priority in physical preparation.

Depending on the climate where you live, you may also want to prepare to provide a source of heat. Since heat and light come from the same fuels, and light usually also produces heat, we are covering these together.

STEP 3: PROVIDE FLASHLIGHTS FOR IMMEDI-ATE USE AND A LONGER-TERM SOURCE OF LIGHT AND HEAT FOR EVENINGS.

Immediately after a disaster, putting out fires and first aid for the injured would be top priorities. However, in this book, we are not looking at priorities of disaster actions; we are looking at priorities of preparation. The next, fourth, priority of preparation is securing adequate first aid supplies. (But you can't give first aid to someone at night without light.)

Chapter 4

FIRST AID FIRST

In these first chapters, we are trying to cover things that would be common to any emergency or disaster, whether coming from nature or being man-made in origin. The reason for this is that you do not know what type of disaster may suddenly hit you. We have seen that the first, and by far most important item of preparation is having a 72-hour survival kit. The second is provision of water. The third most important item to have is light, particularly immediate light from a flashlight right after a disaster, in the event that it occurred at night and you would need to see where the rubble and debris were. If someone were wounded in a disaster, you would need the light in order to see to give that individual proper first aid. This brings us to the fourth step in preparation.

Not only are the knowledge of proper first aid techniques and having on hand adequate first aid supplies essential for emergencies, but they are also very useful in day-to-day living when someone, particularly a child, could hurt himself and require first aid. Believe it or not, children do break bones, get cuts, have scraped knees and elbows and they have even been known to get bitten by a snake or stung by a bee. Some basic understanding of common first aid is certainly a wise thing to acquire. We all need to know how to help someone who has been hurt physically. This knowledge could help you save a life, perhaps the life of someone dear to you.

FIRST AID KNOWLEDGE

In almost every community, the Red Cross and fire departments give first aid and CPR courses. The YMCA and YWCA also give first aid courses and first aid training is available through the Boy Scouts, Girl Scouts and other youth organizations. Also, many hospitals offer first aid courses. The best place to gain the knowledge that you will need to administer proper first aid would be to take one of these courses. It will be time well invested.

We would recommend that, even if you learned basic first aid as a youth, you take one of these courses, not only as a refresher, but because first aid techniques have changed as the medical world has gained knowledge. For example, when I was a youth, we were taught to put butter or some other lubricating substance on a burn. Today, that is known to be absolutely the worst thing to do. You should put something cold on it to absorb the heat and slow the burning process. This can be anything from an ice bag or ice cubes wrapped in a dish towel to some of the modern chemical pouches that will cool when squeezed (available in drugstores). It is also true that the way to administer first aid to various wounds and injuries to the body has changed through the years. You need an update periodically to stay current in order to know exactly what to do. Knowing what to do can help you not to panic, but to act decisively when an emergency does occur, and a level-headed response and action are needed.

One advantage of these courses is that they will give you actual hands-on practice in such things as making a sling for a wounded arm or applying a tourniquet for a wound that is bleeding profusely. They will give you practice in proper bandaging of various areas of the body, and so on. This hands-on experience helps you solidify the knowledge in your mind far better than just watching someone else do it.

However, if it is absolutely impossible for you to attend one of these courses, there are several excellent videos that give this kind of information. Most of these videos are available as community service videos in your local video rental store, but if you cannot find them there, you could contact the producer. The videos that we recommend, which are repeated in Appendix B, are:

"CPR: The Way To Save Lives"
J.D. Heade Company   (800)622-5689

"Fire Safety For The Family"
Academy Entertainment, Inc.   (802)985-2060

"Dr. Heimlich's Home First Aid"
MFA Home Video   (818) 777-4300

"Emergency Action (First Aid)"
Acti Video   (312) 404-0030

"How To Save Your Child's Life"
Xenon Video   (310) 451-5510

But a word of caution—if you use these videos, you ***must*** actually practice on another person (except for CPR) to really make the information yours. One of the video tapes is on the Heimlich Maneuver to unclog the throat if someone is choking. It is not enough to see that done on a video; you ***must*** practice on someone and have the other person practice on you in order to really ***have*** that information. These courses and videos will teach you how to apply first aid to broken bones, wounds, scrapes, burns, and other injuries that you may encounter immediately after a disaster.

However, there is one thing you need to know that really necessitates taking a course. Do not try to learn this from a video. That is CPR. CPR (cardiopulmonary resuscitation) is how to restart someone's heart and breathing if they have stopped. This technique should never be applied to anyone whose heart is still beating, for it can cause severe damage.

The shock of a sudden tornado or earthquake could cause someone to go into cardiac arrest (commonly called a heart attack). Not all heart attacks are fatal and cause the heart to stop, but many do (nearly half). After determining that an individual's heart was no longer beating, you would need to apply CPR immediately to restart his/her heart and breathing if he/she is going to survive.

Some first aid activities, such as CPR, require no supplies. However, treatment of burns, cuts, scrapes, broken bones and many other inquiries requires proper first aid supplies. Having them on hand will give better help faster than if you have to improvise.

FIRST AID SUPPLIES

Every home should have an adequately supplied and *customized* portable first aid box. I do not like the name, "first aid kit" because the image that usually brings to mind for most of us is a little metal box about 4" x 6", which is usually terribly inadequate and can only hold minimal supplies. Actually, a home should have two boxes. One I would call the "medical box" and the other a "first aid box." The "box" may be a ten gallon bucket, a knapsack, a large fishing tackle box, tool box or some other type of container that can easily be grabbed and instantly taken to where an injured person is. If you are in a flood-prone area, these boxes should be waterproof.

The first aid box should be customized to your particular family. For example, if a member of your family has asthma, then one of the breath sprays should be in the box. If one of your family members has heart trouble, perhaps a very small oxygen bottle (miniature ones are available), nitroglycerin tables or spray, and cayenne pepper (which opens up the blood vessels) should be contained in the first aid box. You need to think through the unique problems of your family and build your first aid box around those needs.

In addition to any specialized items that your family would need, the first thing to put in your first aid box is a good first aid handbook, available at most bookstores. You also will need the following:

FIRST AID BOX

FOR BURNS:
Ice Pack   Foile or other First Aid
Water Gel   Spray

SOMETHING IN THE EYE:
Eye drops (such as Visine)   Eye glass to wash eyes
Boric Acid powder to   Eye dropper
    make an eyewash   Q-tips
    (table salt another alternative)

FOR BROKEN BONES:

Small strips of wood for
splints or an inflatable
splint
Adhesive tape

Gauze
Roll of cotton
Material for slings
and dressings

STRAINS AND SPRAINS:

Epsom Salts to reduce
swelling
Melaleuca Pain-A-Trate
(*B)

Ace Bandages
Ice Packs
Melaleuca Mela-Gel
(*B)

FOR CUTS AND SCRAPES:

Sterile 4x4 pads
Antibiotic ointment
Rolls of gauze
Merthiolate (an
antiseptic and
germicide)
Boric Acid (to dilute
for cleansing wounds)
Iodine
Needle and black silk
thread for suturing
(in extreme emergency)
Melaleuca Oil—T36-C7
(*B)

Tourniquet with a twist
stick
Hydrogen peroxide
Baking soda (for insect
bites)
Assorted bandages
(include butterfly
and Band-Aids)
Ethyl Alcohol (rubbing
alcohol)
Melaleuca Mela-Gel
(*B)

FOR INGESTED POISON OR TOXIC SUBSTANCE:

Dry mustard to induce
vomiting
Liquid Charcoal

Syrup of Ipecac to
induce vomiting

OTHER NECESSARY SUPPLIES:

Scissors
One-edged razor blades
Matches

Tweezers
Snake bite kit
Solarcaine

About Melaleuca

Melaleuca is a plant which grows only in Australia. Tea made from the leaves of this plant and an oil pressed from it have been known to have incredible healing and cleansing properties. During World War II, every Australian soldier carried a vial of Melaleuca oil in the first aid kit in his backpack. It was found to be exceptionally effective on burns, skin problems, poisonous insect bites and various fungal and bacterial infections. In addition, it was found to have the following beneficial properties:

Soothing
Natural Antiseptic
Natural Fungicide
Penetrating
Non-Caustic
Aromatic
Natural Solvent

In the defense manufacturing plants in Australia during World War II, they added a little Melaleuca oil to the cutting oil in the factories so that if a worker got cut by a metal particle, it would help the wound not to become infected and fester.

Personally, I would not be without Melaleuca oil in my first aid box. See Appendix B for a source of it.

MEDICINE BOX

The items listed above were for the first aid box. In your family *medical box* you will want to have at least one each of any current prescription medicines needed by any family members. In addition, it would be advisable to include some things to help you physically, so that you can last a few weeks without access to outside medical help. For example, you may wish to include:

Vitamin C	Hot water bottle
Vitamin E	Antacid tablets
Aspirin (a large bottle)	Liquid antacid
Tylenol	(such as Mylanta)
Kaopectate for diarrhea	Cold medicine
Thermometer	Allergy medicine
Sudafed	Cough Medicine
Blistex or Melaleuca lip balm	(Robitussin-DM)

There could be an emergency wherein you have to evacuate your home. Remember, evacuation notices are given by police frequently with hurricane warnings, forest fire warnings, flood warnings, and so forth. If this were to occur, you could throw your medical box and your first aid box in the trunk of your car as you left, knowing that you would have the necessary medical supplies to take care of many first aid needs as well as ongoing health problems.

STEP 4: PREPARE A FIRST AID BOX AND MEDI-CAL BOX, AND LEARN FIRST AID.

Frequently after many types of emergencies or disasters, there is some need for first aid and medical attention that you must give far in advance of any medical professional arriving on the scene, if they arrive at all.

A large fishing tackle box or tool box can handily be used for either the first aid box or medical box. Prepackaged first aid kits usually come with their own box. Some of these boxes are water tight (*B).

Also, after most disasters, there is a problem with fires that must be put out. The big damage in the 1906 earthquake in San Francisco was not done by the earthquake, but by the fires that ensued afterwards. All of the water lines in the city were broken, and there was no water with which to fight these fires.

As any fire-fighting professional knows, a tiny blaze not checked and extinguished can turn into a roaring inferno, as it feeds upon itself. Let us look briefly at the consideration of extinguishing any fires that may occur after a disaster.

Chapter 5

NIP FIRES IN THE BUD

After most disasters, except flooding, a major problem is subsequent fires. Perhaps even more important than rendering first aid is to check for fires that may have started and to extinguish them, before they spread and roar out of control, making your house a fiery inferno. These fires can be caused by downed electrical lines, broken gas lines, spilled gasoline, striking a match to light a cigarette, or a simple spark created by starting an engine or hitting a hoe or other piece of metal on cement.

Of course, the worst case of fire would be after a nuclear explosion. When a nuclear device is detonated, it sends out a wall of fire and heat. At first, that blast wave would move outward, setting on fire many things in its path. Then, almost like the tide that comes up and then recedes, this heat wave would come back into the vacuum that was left from the explosion. This surge of heat and fire out and back can take as long as two minutes. In the table on the next page, you can see the effect of such a wall of fire.

One reason why I strongly recommend the smoke detectors that run from batteries, rather than ones that runs from your household current in most disasters, is because there would be no electricity and your smoke detectors would not work. Yes, I know—it is a lot of trouble to change the batteries every three years, but there is a significant increase in your protection by using battery-powered smoke detectors.

Table 5.1

EFFECTS OF A NUCLEAR EXPLOSION
(Approximate maximum distance from explosion in miles)

Weapon Yield	Fireball Diameter	Severe Damage to Homes	Window Shattering	Paper Ignites	Second Degree Burns
20 KT*	.3	3	4	4	4
100 KT	.6	4	5	5	5
1 MT	1.4	5	9	9	10
5 MT	2.6	6	14	14	17
10 MT	3.5	8	19	23	25
20 MT	4.6	10	24	35	32
30 MT	5.5	12	27	40	40
50 MT	6.6	14	32	50	50
100 MT	9.0	17	41	65	70

KT = Kilotons (1,000 tons of TNT, equivalent)
MT = Megatons (1,000,000 tons of TNT, equivalent)
* = Size of Hiroshima bomb

WHAT MAKES A FIRE

Three things are required to make a fire. These may seem simplistic, but you need to understand them. These things are needed to make a fire:

1. Fuel
2. Oxygen
3. Heat

In the absence of any one of these, a fire will not burn.

You may remember from your childhood the experiment wherein you light a candle, put it in a jar, screw on the lid and watch the flame go out. Remember those fun little games we used to play? What causes the candle to go out? It burns up all the oxygen, and oxygen is necessary to keep a fire going. Perhaps you have been out camping where you had a campfire. When you were leaving, you may have pulled the unburnt pieces of wood off the fire and scattered them around, thus separating the heat from the fuel, and the campfire went out. You may have pitched dirt on top of some of those logs that still had glowing embers. Why did you do that? To cut off the oxygen, so the embers would die out.

Alternatively, you may have thrown a pot of coffee over the glowing coals, as you were ready to put out the campfire. As you poured the coffee on the coals, it sizzled and put up that nice-smelling smoke. This would have reduced the heat, as the water absorbed the heat and turned into steam. If you poured enough water on the coals, the conversion of the water to steam would absorb all the heat and the fire would go out. Therefore, by eliminating any one of the three things necessary to create a fire, you can put out a fire.

EXTINGUISHING A FIRE

You may have wondered where the term "fire fighting" came from. You may not realize it, but when you have an uncontrolled fire, no matter how small, you are in a battle for survival. The fire wants to consume every combustible thing around, and you have to fight it to prevent it from doing just that. Therefore, when you see an uncontrolled fire following a disaster, you should go into "battle mode" with the single goal of extinguishing that fire and keeping it out.

By far the best approach—and the way that most fire fighting is done, particularly with smaller blazes—is to remove the oxygen. If someone's clothes are on fire, you can wrap that person in a blanket, a coat or some such thing that will cut off the oxygen and extinguish the flame. Most fire extinguishers work on this principle. The foam fire extinguishers place a foam over the fire, and the oxygen cannot get down through the foam to the fire. The halogen fire extinguishers, which are very nice for kitchen fires, have a gas that is heavier than air, which comes down over the flame and extinguishes it by cutting off the oxygen supply.

If you are using a water hose to put out a fire, it is best not to have the nozzle directed in a single jet stream, but in a wide umbrella of a fine mist, and bring that fine mist down over the fire. It will extinguish it by cutting off the oxygen supply.

Fires can rage while it is raining. Water alone, in most cases, will not extinguish a fire, unless there is so much water that it reduces the heat to a point below the temperature of ignition.

FIREFIGHTING EQUIPMENT

As we mentioned at the end of the last chapter, the damage done in the 1906 San Francisco earthquake was primarily done by fire, because the water lines were broken and there was no water with which to fight the fires. Frequently, the same thing is true after an earthquake, a hurricane or a tornado. The water supply may be out for days or even weeks. Thus, relying on your handy garden hose to fight a fire is marginal, at best.

This means that you are going to want to have fire extinguishers on hand. You can check with your local fire department as to their recommendation for your type of home and area, and then purchase what they recommend. I would tend to purchase about twice the amount they recommend. If they recommend two fire extinguishers, I would buy four and have them alternately recharged every other year.

I recommend having at least two good quality, commercial-grade, ABC all-purpose fire extinguishers, preferably the 10-pound size. Be sure they have a UL rating of at least 2A 40BC with hose and nozzle.

Another good fire fighting device is sand. You could have boxes, buckets or bags of sand on hand. As of 1993, you could buy gunny sacks or sandbags for 75 cents. You should fill these halfway with sand. They would be good for water control against flooding and also for fighting fires. You would need to have quite a supply of these to be very effective for either purpose. You would probably need to have one wall of your garage stacked about halfway up with these types of bags of sand in order for them to have a great deal of use to you.

Of course, it does not hurt to have garden hoses in the event that there is still water following a disaster. You would want to have a nozzle for that hose designed for fire fighting, one that would give you a nice umbrella of fine spray, as well as a jet stream.

SUMMARY AND CONCLUSION

After almost every major disaster, except flooding, there is a significant danger of fires starting. These may be small fires that you can extinguish before they enlarge and consume your belongings or even your home.

The best way to fight such fires is to cut off the oxygen to them. I recommend having one or more ABC-rated, dry chemical fire extinguishers. For kitchen fires, a halogen fire extinguisher that would cut off the oxygen also would be recommended. Of course, these need to be purchased well in advance; when your house catches on fire, it is a little late to run down and buy a fire extinguisher.

STEP 5: BUY AN ADEQUATE NUMBER OF FIRE EXTINGUISHERS AND ACQUAINT FAMILY MEMBERS WITH THEIR LOCATION AND HOW TO USE THEM.

We have covered the early essentials for surviving an emergency: having a 72-hour survival kit, having water to drink, and with which to cook; having light, so that you can see to exit a building or give first aid; having the tools to give first aid to any injured people; and having the proper equipment to extinguish any fires, as well as being very careful not to start a fire. With these preparations, you now have a good chance to survive the initial period of time after a disaster.

There is a subject that we need to discuss. That is preparation for violence because, after most emergencies, there could well be rioting and looting. Also, you could encounter violence just walking down a street or someone could break into your home even during regular times, aside from disasters. Unfortunately, most people are not prepared for violence.

Chapter 6

BEING ALERT FOR VIOLENCE

Up until now in this book, we have been looking at emergencies and disasters that are community-wide. Those that nature would cause would include earthquakes, volcanic eruptions, tornadoes, hurricanes and flooding. We have also discussed fire to a certain extent, which could affect the entire community after an earthquake. Fire could also be a potential hazard for homes near forested and rural areas or really any home could be threatened without forewarning. We need to realize that these types of disasters could strike us at any time, almost at any place. As I look at the projections by climatologists for the coming years, as well as considering geologic trends and probabilities, my forecast would be that we are entering an era of progressively heavier violence from nature.

In this chapter, I would like to switch from considering violent acts of nature and widespread violent acts of men, such as nuclear war, and move on to consider violence toward an individual. There could conceivably be an individual attack against you or members of your family by thieves, muggers, terrorists, kidnappers, or rioters. As violence and terrorism increase worldwide, we need to be prepared mentally and otherwise for personal violence.

THE FOUR CONDITIONS

There are four conditions of alertness (which the military uses) in which a person can find himself. I have seen these same categories used by other writers to mean various things, but I would like to give you my definitions of them.

Condition White: When you are in "condition white," you are completely relaxed. There is basically no alertness to any potential danger. It is a very oblivious condition.

Condition Yellow: In this condition, you become alert to any potential danger that you might encounter. There is no tenseness, but there is a mental alertness when you are in "condition yellow." If there were to be a sudden sound or movement, your state of alertness would cause you to be ready to act.

Condition Orange: You shift from "condition yellow" to "condition orange" when there appears to be a danger present that can harm property or person. This property might be your home, automobile, wallet, purse, or any other of your possessions and the person could be yourself, a loved one or anyone else present.

Condition Red: This is the heightened condition you go into when there is a pressing danger and imminent harm could come to your person, property, or the bodies of people about whom you are concerned.

Unfortunately, most people spend much or even most of their time in condition white. They are unaware of any potential dangers that might be around, whether from nature or from man. And even if they vaguely think about them, many tend to assume that someone else will take care of the danger and protect them.

There are other people who are usually in condition yellow, particularly when they are working. One example of this is a pilot. When I took my pilot training, we checked our gauges and dials about every 30 seconds and we were trained to continually ask ourselves, "If the engine quit now, where would we set this baby down?" At one point, the answer might be, "On that golf course." A few minutes later, the answer might be, "On that highway" or "In that farmer's field." Pilots must be continually in condition yellow, alert to any possible dangers, planning the actions that they will take if danger materializes.

While I was taking flying instruction, I once dropped one of the charts on the floor of the plane. I bent down to pick it up, and was about halfway down when I raised back up quickly and pulled the nose of the plane up. When the instructor asked me why I did that, I said, "The sound of the motor changed, and I could tell we were beginning to fall." This is an example of being in condition yellow continually, which is a necessity when you are in any potentially hazardous situation like flying.

There are other professions that require their people to constantly be in condition yellow while at work. One example of this might be a doctor or nurse. Crises, big or small, can occur with patients at any time, whether it be in a maternity ward, a critical care ward, an operating room, or even one of the regular wards. These health care professionals are constantly on the alert for danger signs. They are trained in what specific actions to take when those danger signs occur and the danger appears to be real.

I find it a helpful exercise to periodically check to see which condition I am in—white, yellow, orange, or red. Personally, I am seldom in condition white. Even when sitting at home relaxing and watching a movie, if there is an unusual noise around the ranch, I am very much on the alert to check it out and to take appropriate action, if necessary. I know many other people who are never in condition white, but always remain in condition yellow.

Some readers might think that this is a militaristic, warlike, red-neck type of attitude to remain basically in condition yellow. Yet, if we take a look at the Bible, it is interesting to see that this is a biblical principle. When God told Gideon to choose an army, several thousand people appeared. As a test to see who was really qualified, Gideon asked them all to take a drink from the river. Most of the people ran down to the river and stuck their faces into the water, totally oblivious to any potential danger (they were in condition white), and they were rejected from further consideration. Those who scooped some water up into their hands, and drank from their hands while surveying the horizon were the ones chosen for the army. These chosen people were constantly in condition yellow. They were not "worried" about danger nor petrified by the thought of it, but they wanted to be alert to it in the event that it came their direction.

A practical application of utilizing yellow condition would be a typical family camping trip. Just about everyone enjoys a family campout at sometime, and unfortunately we all-too-often take our "condition white" mentality along. Our daily life in the "civilized" world, with its built-in protective environment (however flimsy that may be in reality) can lull us into a perpetually-relaxed mental state. Even though we go camping for relaxation and recreation, we must remember that when we walk away from "home" and into the woods or wilderness, we are leaving a complex set of life-support systems and entering a survival type of situation that is generally underestimated.

Many unfortunate hunting and camping accidents happen because people are in condition white while out in the woods. For example, if there is a fallen tree, many people will nonchalantly step over it, not realizing that snakes love to stretch out parallel to fallen tree trunks. By stepping over it with no awareness of potential danger, they invite a snake bite from a startled snake. (One should step on top of a fallen tree and then take a giant step over and away from it. If in condition yellow and aware of the potential danger, one will do this.)

Similarly, in areas where there are regular flash floods, people in condition white have been known to choose a campsite in a river bed, because it was nice and sandy and there was not any brush to clear. They subsequently drowned in a flash flood when a wall of water ten feet high came down and covered them and their camp. Certainly, campsites should be chosen while in condition yellow, looking for potential danger from flash floods, from a campfire setting a tree on fire, from rocks falling from an overhanging ledge, and so forth. I think you get the general idea that, particularly when we are in a strange environment, such as the woods, I believe it is essential to stay in condition yellow.

My general observation is that most people spend far too much time in condition white and are not alert to potential danger, either from nature or from man.

SHIFTING TO
CONDITION ORANGE OR RED

Nature has a way of doing some of the shifting for us from condition orange to condition red. When a real danger to our property or person is present, our adrenalin starts flowing, and our body gets us ready for either "fight or flight." This usually is an automatic, biological response, given to us by God, over which we have no control.

However, when this happens, the average person has not thought through any predetermined plans of action for responding to a crisis. Even with adrenalin pumping, he will tend to stand there, frozen while he is trying to make a decision as to whether he should fight or run. If he makes the decision to fight, he also must to decide what to fight with and whether or not he is really willing to hurt his attacker, and so forth. Hundreds of decisions run through his mind, basically immobilizing him and causing him to be subject to harm.

As I noted earlier, an airplane pilot is continually asking himself, "If my engines quit, where will I set this plane down?" A nurse may be thinking, "If the heart stops, I will immediately go to CPR or the electrical stimulator." A wise automobile driver has thought through in advance what he will do if his brakes fail. For example, he might plan first to turn off the ignition to see if the engine will stop the car. If that does not work, he may plan to sacrifice the transmission for protection of his person and property by shifting either into low or reverse. Some drivers occasionally pretend their brakes have gone out and turn off the ignition just to see how their cars will respond and how long it takes to stop, so that when they have a real emergency, they will know which action is most appropriate to take.

The preferable and intelligent way to shift from condition yellow into either condition orange or red is to have "preplanned" as much as possible the specific actions that you will take when a particular danger presents itself.

ARE YOU WILLING
TO HARM AN ATTACKER?

You notice the question was not, "Do you *want* to harm an attacker?" I think that only sadistic individuals *want* to harm people. The real question is: Are you *willing* to harm someone, if you or a loved one is attacked or your property is attacked? I do not have *"the answer"* to that for everyone, as we discuss in Chapter 7 dealing with protecting your stored food. I have met people who would approach this question from completely opposite directions.

There are those who say, "In no way do I want to get physically involved in protecting property." If a robber comes into their store, some owners would say, "Take all the money in the cash register; it's insured, and I'm not going to try to stop you." Others, with the same conclusions about property, say that if they were to discover a robber in their house, they would let him take what he wanted rather than risk any physical harm. Similarly, some women have concluded that if their purse is snatched, they will not risk being harmed over a purse. Some have even decided not to resist a rape attack because of the risk of getting hurt or killed.

Others have taken the opposite point of view and feel that their property is a very private, important thing to them, and they are willing to shoot or even to kill a robber who is trying to take their personal possessions. I receive a lot of unusual things in the mail. Recently, someone sent me a decal, that I guess people could put on their doors and windows, that contains the following message:

THE OWNER OF THIS PROPERTY IS ARMED AND IS WILLING AND ABLE TO PROTECT IT. THERE IS NOTHING IN HERE WORTH DYING FOR.

As you can see, people of this mentality, who post such notices, are ready to defend their property to the nth degree.

One must consider that there is property and then there is property. If someone is going to take a television set, that is one thing. But if there is a nationwide famine, or food shortage because of a trucker's or railroad strike, and someone comes in to steal your last two months' worth of food, then taking your food may be very analogous to trying to harm your body. Potentially, if he took all of your food and you were left without any, you and your family could indeed starve to death.

This takes us to the question, what if there is a mugger, a kidnapper or a terrorist who appears with the obvious intent of harming you physically or even killing you? Or what if someone appears with a knife or a gun and is coming in your direction, or is moving menacingly toward a member of your family or someone else close to you? Most people, if they stop and think about it, are willing to risk some bodily harm in order to protect themselves or their loved ones from major physical harm or death.

I am not for nor against the use of defensive violence to meet danger. What I do feel is that a person should carefully think through what he is or is not willing to do, once he shifts from condition yellow or orange to red. It may be that he would like to be able to do some things for which he does not have the skill or equipment, such as karate or shooting. By predetermining what he wants to do, he can take appropriate training, if necessary.

MILD METHODS OF SELF-DEFENSE

The mildest form of defense is to flee. In the face of danger, there is nothing cowardly about running and attempting to avoid physical confrontation. If a woman being accosted is on a street, she should not walk fast but literally *run* to a store, a policeman, or someone who can help. Once I was on a subway in New York late at night, and a suspicious-looking character got on the car with me. He may have been perfectly innocent, but I felt evil coming from him, so I simply got up and moved to a different car.

Unfortunately, in many instances, it seems we have become a nation of sheep, and many people would not even run if danger were to present itself. There was a case concerning a lady who stopped at a red light very late at night. A burly character opened her car door and got in, subsequently doing her some physical harm, including rape. When asked why she did not press hard on the accelerator the moment he opened the car door, her response was, "The light was still red." Even though there were no cars coming in either direction, she sat there and allowed the man to get into the car, because she did not want to run a red light.

We must remember that in times of danger, the rules can change, and probably it would have been a good idea to have run that red light. Unfortunately, when the woman got into her car, she was in condition white. If she had been in condition yellow, driving that late and alone at night, she would have at least locked the doors. We see that one can flee, even when in an automobile. In her case, I am sure you would agree that the price of a ticket for running a red light would have been well worth it.

You need to think through beforehand how much harm you are willing to do to a person who physically attacks you.

Another thing you could do would be to have a cellular telephone or a CB radio in your car. I realize that the CB craze has passed, but a lady on a lonely road with a flat tire could find that a CB radio will usually bring help. (CB's have a much wider range than cellular telephones.) Calling for help is much safer than if she were to try to get out and change the tire herself or walk along a dark road to a service station. She could ask those listening on their CB to assist her. Many CBers would have heard the cry for help, and it is unlikely that one bad one would try to take advantage of the situation, because he would know that possibly others were on their way who had also heard the call for help.

MEDIUM METHODS OF SELF-DEFENSE

If one decides that passive methods of defense, such as running from danger or having a cellular telephone or a CB radio to call for help, are insufficient preparations, and if one decided that he is willing to do a mild amount of bodily harm to an attacker, there are other things that can be very helpful. For example, many things that people frequently have with them can be excellent weapons. The corner of a book can be a very potent weapon, when jabbed into someone's solar plexus or face. Similarly, a rattail comb or a key can be used as a weapon. Fingernails gouging into a person's face and eyes are very powerful weapons. In addition, every person carries with him ten very able weapons. They are: two hands, two elbows, two feet, two knees, one head, and one mouth. It is unlikely that an attacker can immobilize all ten of your weapons at once. You will have at least one of them with which to fight back and defend yourself.

Your most potent weapons are your hands. When an attacker grabs you by the arm, the throat, around the chest, or wherever, if you simply grasp his little finger and pull back until it breaks, he will be temporarily immobilized from the pain. Unfortunately, many people are so conditioned that they would allow severe harm to come to their person rather than break an attacker's finger. Similarly, a hard step down on the arch of an attacker's foot can break his arch and render him immobile. You will usually have your feet free, and this is something that can be done in almost every situation.

Obviously, there are many other things that one could do that we will not attempt to cover here. Just be aware that you have many very potent weapons with you at all times, and your attacker has many very vulnerable places on his body. But what you are *willing* to do if attacked should be predecided.

Another medium method of defense would be a chemical spray, such as mace, tear gas or pepper gas (OC, oleoresin capsicum). Of these, pepper gas (OC) is more effective. In fact, many police departments are now converting to it from tear gas. Regardless of your size, you can stop an aggressive attacker three times your size with these pepper gas sprays.

The key to OC is its inflammatory nature. Whereas tear gasses rely on a subject's ability to feel pain (irritant), OC causes swelling of the mucus tissues of the eyes, nose, throat and upper respiratory tract. The effects of the spray are instantaneous and cause the attacker's eyes to swell shut, breathing capacity to be reduced to life support levels, coughing, choking and nausea. It becomes virtually impossible to continue any aggressive behavior. All symptoms disappear within thirty to forty-five minutes with no aftereffects or permanent damage. This will also have the same effect on animals. It is probably the ideal self-defense weapon for most Christians, but you must have one with you for it to work. You will probably need several to ensure that you have one handy, one for your purse or coat pocket, one for your bedside, one at work and so forth. The OC aerosol sprays Bodyguard, On-Guard or Escort are recommended (*B).

For further information on this entire subject, there are two videos mentioned in Appendix B on self-defense that I would highly recommend.

STRONG METHODS OF SELF-DEFENSE

Most of the strong methods of self-defense require some type of training. These would include one of the martial arts, such as karate, or the use of weapons.

There was a case of a young lawyer leaving his law firm in New York City late at night. Three muggers attacked him. This lawyer happened to have been well along in karate training. He flattened all three of them and stood over them daring any of them to get up while the police came. (Very shortly after that, all of the lawyers in his firm decided they would study karate.)

Karate does not depend on one's size. There is a 100-pound lady who is teaching karate to the Marines, and she has no challengers among her 6-foot-plus students. The martial arts can be utilized as good physical conditioning exercise, as well as providing some means of self-defense. One does not have to get into martial arts philosophy or false religion or become "militant," in order to learn simple self-defense. Many of the YMCA's and YWCA's have very good self-defense programs for both men and women.

An even stronger method of self-defense, when facing imminent danger, is the use of weapons. There are a number of types of weapons, such as crossbows, airbows (propelled by compressed CO_2 or air) and high-powered air rifles, but when most people think of defending themselves with a weapon, they are referring to a gun of some type, usually a handgun, shotgun or a rifle.

If one were only going to purchase one gun, I believe that it should be a handgun. After a great deal of research, I have changed my mind on which are the best handguns for defense. I have concluded that they are either a .45-caliber semiautomatic or a 9 mm semiautomatic. Rifles and shot guns have an advantage of a longer range, but they can be awkward at close range (despite what you might think from watching "The Rifleman" TV series). However, there are a number of words of caution in using such weapons.

First, a person should be well trained in its use and comfortable with it. There are a number of places where one can get such training. Probably the best known and most reputable one is Gunsite training school in Arizona, originally founded by Jeff Cooper (*B).

In past years, among his students, Jeff has had judges, doctors and lawyers, as well as many high-ranking officials from foreign countries. They learn to use weapons effectively from all positions. He has a room called "The Playhouse," where figures pop out, both "good guys" and "bad guys." One is taught to shoot the bad guys and not the good guys.

The son of the head of a Latin American country went through the training at Gunsite. A few months later his car was curbed by a car full of six husky men, evidently intent upon capturing him and possibly killing him. After being curbed, he jumped out of his car, rolled across the street, drawing his .45 as he rolled, and shot all six of his attackers before they could even get their weapons out of their holsters.

The son of this Latin American leader was always in condition yellow, and when condition red occurred, he had preplanned his actions and could and did execute them swiftly and with precision.

I am not necessarily advocating this type of self-defense in the average situation. But if an individual is going to rely on a handgun as a defensive tool, he needs to be able to use it with proficiency; otherwise, he would have a false security. Some people feel a gun is their security, but when a crisis comes, they are not able to use it.

TURN THE OTHER CHEEK?

The courts and laws of this land say that to harm or even kill in self-defense is alright. Since killing someone is a moral question, we need to turn to the Bible for some help.

There are some Christians who feel that you should not defend yourself nor your property. There are others who go so far as to suggest that you should not even defend your country in a time of war. They primarily base this belief on something Jesus said in the Sermon on the Mount:

38 "You have heard that it was said, 'An eye for an eye, and a tooth for a tooth.'

39 "But I say to you, do not resist him who is evil; but whoever slaps you on your right cheek, turn to him the other also.

40 "And if anyone wants to sue you, and take your shirt, let him have your coat also.

41 "And whoever shall force you to go one mile, go with him two...."

—Matthew 5

29 "Whoever hits you on the cheek, offer him the other also; and whoever takes away your coat, do not withhold your shirt from him either.

30 "Give to everyone who asks of you, and whoever takes away what is yours, do not demand it back...."

—Luke 6

Based on this teaching, I have heard Christian men say that regardless of what someone was doing to a member of their family, even raping their wife and stabbing her to death, they would not try to hit or restrain the man. People are certainly entitled to hold this position, but it is wise to have thought and prayed through the issue beforehand to be sure that is exactly what they intend to do in such a situation. It is a position I honestly would have difficulty holding.

There are other Christians who feel that it is alright to defend one's person, family and property. They base this on a subsequent teaching of Jesus:

35   And He said to them, "When I sent you out without purse and bag and sandals, you did not lack anything, did you?" And they said, "*No*, nothing."

36   And He said to them, "But now, let him who has a purse take it along, likewise also a bag, and let him who has no sword sell his robe and buy one...."
—Luke 22

In the New Testament days, one's robe was one of his most priceless possessions. As people traveled and slept along the roadside, this was what they wrapped themselves in at night. In fact, the Old Testament law says that you could not keep a man's robe overnight. But, as precious as the robe was, Jesus told His disciples to sell it and buy a sword. Some conclude that there was no reason for Jesus to tell His disciples to buy a sword, unless they would be trained and ready to use it in their defense.

Christians who think self-defense is appropriate also consider another teaching of Jesus:

34   "Do not think that I came to bring peace on the earth; I did not come to bring peace, but a sword...."
—Matthew 10

They also point out the fact that the Bible says God does not change—He is the same yesterday, today, and forever. As the Israelites conquered the promised land, they did so by the sword. This was not even done in defense; this was an offensive military action. Then there was David who not only killed Goliath with his sword, but later killed tens of thousands of Israel's enemies. Those of this persuasion contend that if God does not change, and if He approved of these actions by Joshua, David, and many others, God would still approve of violence in certain situations today.

One thing we should note is that there is a different Hebrew word for *murder* than there is for *kill.* The Hebrew word used in the sixth commandment of the Ten Commandments is the word for *murder.* All of the modern translations (*NKJV, NAS, NIV, NRSV*) say:

13 "You shall not murder...."

—Exodus 20

There is a passage in Numbers 35:16-29 that explains the difference between killing and murder. God would not have commanded Joshua to kill all the people at Jericho if that would contradict the Ten Commandments.

Just as with other controversial subjects within the Scriptures, there is ample Biblical evidence for both sides. The main point is that one needs to decide ahead of time whether to defend or stand by. Trying to make that decision when harm is imminent is the wrong time to make it.

SUMMARY AND CONCLUSION

Let's see where we have come thus far. Times appear to be becoming more violent. This violence can come from nature in the form of things such as volcanoes, earthquakes, tidal waves, tornadoes, hurricanes, and flooding. There are certain things which were discussed in earlier chapters of this book that one can do to prepare for these natural acts of violence.

Obviously, to any intelligent observer, the acts of terrorism, hostage taking, and violent crime are on the rise in America and in the world today. One of the reasons that many people are susceptible to these acts of violence against their person and property is because they are in condition white too much of the time. Simply spending more time in condition yellow would allow an individual to avoid many of these situations or to nip them in the bud when they arise, by fleeing or removing oneself from the area of potential violence. For example, when one sees a large crowd gathering outside a building, he could leave and return at a later time, after any potential demonstrations or other problems are over. At the American Embassy in Teheran, those who fled did not become hostages.

Another thing that most people basically have not done is to develop a predetermined plan of action to take when they shift from condition yellow to condition orange or red in the face of certain kinds of danger. It would be wise to take lessons from the pilots, doctors, nurses, wise automobile drivers, and other professionals, and to develop predetermined plans of action for crisis situations.

One of the major decisions to be made in developing a predetermined plan of action is to decide how far you will go in protecting yourself or your property (or those persons dear to you). For example, what would you do if someone were to come up to you with a knife pointed at you and demand your purse or wallet? That is not generally the best time to start thinking through your options. Once the decision is made about what actions you are willing to take in self defense, it may be that appropriate training will be necessary in order to have the skills to follow through with your predetermined plan of action for condition orange or condition red situations. The more a person can think through his choices and preferred actions in certain types of crises ahead of time, the better off he will be.

STEP 6: DECIDE HOW MUCH HARM, IF ANY, YOU WOULD BE WILLING TO DO TO AN ATTACKER AND BUY ANY NECESSARY ITEMS OR ACQUIRE ANY NEEDED TRAINING.

I would recommend that you list possible situations in one column and in a column next to that write down the action you would take if that event occurred. Remember that some of the actions you might take could bring on a lawsuit. But it is probably better to be alive and be sued.

Now that we have looked briefly at preparation for violence, let us consider a subject that is vital to us all—food. Up to now we have not discussed the subject of food storage, other than having some short-term emergency reserves for quick energy in your 72-hour kit. However, there are many possible situations in which you would need to provide food for yourself and your family for many weeks, perhaps months after an emergency. So in the next chapter we will examine food storage, food preparation, and food preservation.

The reason we have placed long-term food storage much lower on the priority list than some advisors would is because most people can go without any food, just with water, for forty days without any physical harm. In fact, a ten-day fast can be very beneficial to your body. This important subject will also be discussed in the next chapter.

So do not panic if you have no food. But the ideal is to have some, so let us now examine the important consideration of food storage.

Chapter 7

FOOD, FOOD, GLORIOUS FOOD

We have tried to take these emergency preparations in order of priority. I have saved the subject of food as the last of the seven major essentials in preparing for emergencies. One could validly argue that it should come before some of the others. I would not disagree that it could be Step 6. I have placed it as number 7 for a reason:

1. 72-Hour Survival Kits
2. Water Storage and Purification
3. Light and Heat Sources
4. First Aid and Medical Boxes
5. Firefighting Equipment
6. Self Defense
7. Food Storage

Most books I have seen on preparing for emergencies start with food. In fact, one excellent little book, *A Beginner's Guide To Family Preparedness,* has five full chapters and part of the sixth, out of seven chapters in the book, devoted to food. There is only one chapter that does not deal with food.

Why do I say food is less important? Because the average person can go ten to forty days with no food without any significant problems.

LET'S EXAMINE FASTING

When I say that the average person can go without food for ten days to forty days, I am talking about fasting, where one only drinks water and does not eat any foods nor drink fruit or vegetable juices. Fasting is not man's idea; it is God's idea, and in the Bible He actually commands it. Here I need to refer to the book of wisdom a bit, the Bible, so stay with me. Fasting is taught all through the Old Testament. And in the New Testament, Jesus said that after He left the earth, His disciples would fast (Matthew 9:14,15).

We will deal with food storage later in this chapter, but first we need to take a serious look at fasting, because it is important to understand for our discussion at hand. Immediately after Jesus Christ was baptized, He went out into the wilderness and fasted for forty days. What most people do not realize is that after about the first two days, all hunger disappears. The Bible tells us that *"after* the forty days were completed, Jesus became hungry" (Matthew 4:2).   For the majority of His fast, He had no hunger.

For many reasons, I would recommend a fast to anyone, whether he is a Christian, or religious or not. It is one way the body has of cleansing itself of toxins that we have taken in through the years (such as the residual insecticidal spray on an apple). In addition, fasting gives many of our organs a rest so that they can rejuvenate themselves. Perhaps this is why God created us in such a way that we can fast and why He commanded it.

Because there is confusion on the subject, I would like to briefly address the details of a fast.

Fasting for Renewal

It is possible that in a time of emergency, we may need to fast for several days, maybe even ten, twenty, or forty days. During a time of emergency, when stress would be high anyway, that is *not* the time to try your *first* fast. I would recommend that the entire family go on a fast well beforehand, so that even the children can experience the benefits of a fast and not become panicky when they have no food. The problem with most people in America is not that they have too little food, but that they have too much.

One recent survey showed that 80 percent of Americans are overweight by an average of 20 pounds. As I travel to speak, it is my observation that most groups tend to reflect those same statistics. We need to be toned up and to eliminate that "excess baggage." There could well be some changes in dietary habits that are necessary for us.

I recommend a ten-day fast, unless there are medical reasons why you should do otherwise. However, for the average normal, healthy individual, a ten-day fast should be no problem. If you ask most doctors if you should fast, they will likely say "no," since the benefits of fasting were probably not taught as a part of their traditional medical training. Instead, ask your doctor if there is any biological reason why you could not go on a ten-day fast. In most cases, there will not be any reason why you could not fast.

One other point worth mentioning here is that many people who drink coffee are addicted to the caffeine, whether or not they realize it. Coming off of coffee can produce tremendous headaches and other physical withdrawal symptoms. I encourage a person who drinks coffee to stop drinking it one week before he starts a fast. This way he will go through the physical discomfort from the coffee (caffeine) withdrawal, without confusing those sensations with fasting. Since it is the caffeine that is addictive, this would also apply to heavy drinkers of tea and colas, which also contain significant amounts of caffeine.

Now let us discuss the mechanics of fasting. There are four distinct phases to a fast which are as follows:

PHASE ONE: This is the "gearshift" phase. About forty-eight hours after you eat your last meal, the pituitary gland will begin to emit a hormone that will tell your body to take its energy from its stored energy rather than from incoming food. During these first two or three days, you may have a bit of nausea, dizziness, headaches or weakness. Don't worry; this is normal. All of the toxins that you have taken in (such as any insecticide residues on the skin of fruits or vegetables, chemical additives, etc.) in excess of what your body has been able to eliminate are stored in the fat cells of your body. Your body has only five ways to eliminate toxins: through the lymph, urine, bowel movements, perspiration and your breath. Generally, within about twenty-four hours after you start fasting, your bowel movements will stop. At that point, the primary ways that you will be eliminating toxins—some of which may have been stored in your body for many years—will be through your urine and your breath. Thus, you may experience very bad breath during the first part or even all of your fast. Jeani and I carry a little spray bottle of breath freshener with us during a fast and use it occasionally, both for our sake and for the sake of others.

PHASE TWO: This phase is short and you will tend to experience a bit of weakness that usually only lasts about a day. The energy that is stored is not quite the caliber of the energy from food you take in and, thus, for the remainder of your fast, you will likely be operating on about 80 percent of your normal energy level, but we have found that we still have plenty of energy to do our regular work. After phase two is over, all hunger will disappear. Many who fast for just one or two days at a time have never made it over this "hump" where hunger disappears.

PHASE THREE: The remainder of the fast, days four through ten (or even up to day forty, if God is so directing you) is a time of physical cleansing, as you give your digestive system a rest in order to repair itself and let your body rejuvenate itself. Also, after about the seventh day of the fast, you will find a heightened spiritual awareness. If you are one who reads the Bible and prays, you will very likely find that these times will become more anointed than you have ever found them to be and you may find that God begins to speak to you in a more direct and clear way. You may be surprised at how good you feel. What a wonderful experience this is! You will likely also find that you will lose about a pound each day for the first week or so. This rapid rate of weight loss will decline as the fast continues.

PHASE FOUR: This is the phase of breaking the fast. You want to come off your fast gently and gradually. Your first meal may be a glass of fruit or vegetable juice, diluted 50 percent with water. You can then gradually begin to add a little bit of solid food. Fresh fruit is a good thing to start with when you reintroduce solid foods, as it digests very quickly and easily. Dairy products, such as cheese, are not good to eat initially. Treat your body gently as it is coming off this fast and add quantity to your meals gradually, until you are back up to the meal size that you should eat. (You may find that you do not need to eat meals that are as large as you previously ate, once your system is cleansed and you are better able to digest your food.) Don't go from fasting to gluttony. Coming off of your fast properly is very important; be careful.

For most of us, our body is really a spoiled brat. We generally give it about anything it wants, when it comes to eating. Many people who are trying to live lives that are moral and pleasing to God don't commit adultery, don't drink, and don't take dope, but boy can they eat! They walk around with a big girth advertising to the world: "Look, I'm yielding to lust of the flesh. I overeat routinely." Like any other spoiled brat, you cannot begin to discipline gradually; the iron curtain must fall. Fasting is the "rod" that will tame the spoiled brat that is your body.

For some, the first extended fast (four days or more) is a little more difficult than subsequent ones. Others do not even have the hunger pangs during the first two or three days of subsequent fasts. If you find more physical discomfort than you expected during your first extended fast, do not be alarmed; many people do. If you do experience dizziness, weakness, nausea, headaches and so forth during the first few days of your fast, it is probably just your body getting rid of a high level of toxins.

Many people have had physical problems healed during a fast. I had hypoglycemia prior to my first ten-day fast. During the ten-day fast, either biologically or by a miracle of God, my hypoglycemia was cured. Perhaps for the first time in my life, my body had a chance to stabilize the blood sugar level and keep it stable for awhile. But in general, it is a healing time for your body, as it is detoxified, purified, and cleansed.

Let me hasten to clarify that I am certainly not against eating; in fact, I enjoy it a lot myself (probably too much).

We will now turn from the discussion of fasting to various considerations about food during times of emergency. You may choose to eat during a time of emergency for the extra energy that you might need in order to handle the stress. The reason for including fasting first is so that you will not panic if you are caught someplace away from the food that you have stored and have to exist on a rudimentary level for several days. By becoming familiar and comfortable with fasting now, you will be totally convinced that missing a few meals is no big thing. But it is obviously desirable to be able to provide food for yourself during an emergency. So let us now take a look at that important topic.

THE BASIC COMPONENTS
OF A FOOD STORAGE PROGRAM

Food storage is certainly not something new. During the six thousand years of recorded history, people have been storing up food that they produced during times of plenty for use during the winter or during times when food was scarce. Many of our grandparents would can and preserve foods that they grew on their farms. Often they would have a root cellar for storing vegetables, they would cure meat by smoking it, and so forth. These were all methods of storing food for the time when it was needed. Only in the last twenty to fifty years has the storing of food been forgotten by most people in the industrialized nations. I would suggest that it is time to return to this activity which proved so beneficial for many thousands of years.

Today, in regard to a food storage program for the average U.S. family, we are looking at six basic types of food for storage:

1. Wet pack food—everyday foods that you buy in the grocery store.
2. Frozen foods.
3. Air-dried (dehydrated) foods.
4. Freeze-dried foods.
5. No Cook and MRE meals.
6. Bulk storage of basic foods such as wheat, rice, beans, powdered milk, honey and salt.

You can develop a low cost food storage program. We give the details of it later in this chapter. But first, let us look at an overall comprehensive program. The ideal would be for a family to have a three-month supply of wet pack and frozen foods, and at least a twelve-month supply of air-dried and freeze-dried dehydrated foods. Some families may want to add the bulk storage of some basic foods to this. Let's examine these categories one at a time.

Wet Pack and Frozen Foods for Storage

First, let's be sure we agree on what is meant by "wet pack." By this, I refer to all the items that you find in a supermarket, such as canned fruits, vegetables, meats, cereals, grains, flour, sugar, and prepackaged meals. Wet pack includes items that are packaged for everyday use in the home, without being especially prepared for long-term storage, as well as home canned foods.

A major advantage of wet pack foods is that you are used to preparing them for your family and they are comfortable eating these foods. In an emergency, your family would hardly notice the change in their diet. A major disadvantage is the fact that the maximum storage life of most of these foods is one to two years. Another problem is storage space; a year's supply of wet pack foods for a family of five would take up 60 percent of a two-car garage.

But disadvantages aside, wet pack is an excellent way to build up your storage to a two- or three-month supply. If you do this wisely, you can be sure that none of it will spoil. It can be stored in cupboards in your kitchen and in a small part of your garage.   Also, you can build your supply in small increments that fit easily into your budget. For example, each week you could buy eight days worth of food, instead of just enough for seven days.

The important thing to remember is to buy the items that you *use* frequently, and in quantities that you can use up in a maximum of three months. Too often I find people buying cases of "specials" for their storage which they then allow to sit unused on shelves, until they spoil, because they are not the brand that the family usually uses, or because the amount stored is far more than the family uses in a year. While it is wise to look for the best bargains, it is foolish to buy something just because it is on sale. A good way to build up your supply is to buy an extra can or two each time you go shopping. Soon you will find your supply growing and you will hardly notice the difference in your grocery bill.

Food should be stored in the coolest possible places. Never store your supply in the attic, in the top of a garage, in a heater room or over a stove. The cooler the food is kept, the longer it will keep. Items that are packaged in paper sacks or boxes should not be stored where there are pungent odors, as they will pick up odors. Try not to store your food in deep cabinets where items can be pushed to the back and left to spoil, because they are inconvenient to get out and use. If you store the containers on the floor, it is best to put two-by-fours under them to allow air to circulate and prevent odors from being absorbed from the floor.

You can increase the storage life of canned foods, such as fruits, vegetables, and meats, by turning them upside down periodically to let the juices run back through the product. In some cases this will double the shelf life of the items that you store. However, *if you are storing large quantities of wet pack food, it is best to date the cans or cases and to be sure to use them in date sequence.* This is wise even if your storage of wet pack is small.

Flour is one of the hardest items to store. It will almost always wither, turn dark and taste strange, or hatch weevils. The best way I have found to store flour is to put it into tightly-sealed plastic containers with a layer of bay leaves every 3 inches. This seems to help retain the flavor, stops it from packing and stops insect growth. Even with these precautions, flour should be stored no longer than eighteen months.

When you open a package of powdered milk, reseal the container and put the unused portion in the refrigerator to help prevent it from turning rancid before you get to the bottom of the package.

Fats and oils are food items that are difficult to store long term. They do not keep well because light, oxygen and heat destroy the delicate chemical bonds. Olive oil is the most stable oil and will keep for up to two years in a cool and closed container, and it should be used up within nine months after you have opened it. Oils such as safflower and sunflower oils will keep for up to a year in a cool and closed container, and they should be used up within three months after opening. Vegetable shortening powders or dehydrated butter are available from dehydrated food companies. Another thing to keep in mind concerning fats is that essential fatty acids can be obtained in the form of whole foods, where the fats are kept intact, through grinding your own grains, beans and seeds.

When storing frozen foods, a top-opening freezer is preferable. As you know, hot air rises and cold air sinks. When you open the door of a vertical-opening freezer, the cold air comes pouring out; but with a top-opening freezer, the cold air stays in. If you had no electricity for several days (with which to run your freezer), as happens in many emergency situations, this could mean the difference in keeping your foods frozen or not.

Air-Dried Dehydrated Foods for Storage

Wet pack foods have a shelf life of about two years. After that time, they begin to deteriorate in nutritional value, and frequently the cans will become puffy. The food may remain edible longer than that. However, my experience has been that you cannot *depend* on canned food for longer than two years.

There are many companies today producing air-dried dehydrated food for a longer-term storage. This food is usually packed in the large number 10 cans and it has a shelf life of at least ten years. It also has significant advantages over wet pack food, in that it weighs much less and is about one-fourth the volume (size) of wet pack food. Enough dehydrated food to feed an individual for a year can be stored in a space that is 36 inches by 18 inches. To many men and women who were in the service, the phrase "dehydrated food" brings back very unpleasant memories. However, the current dehydrated foods are delicious and, in most cases, indistinguishable from wet pack foods, when prepared properly.

Most of these food companies have various prearranged groups of food that would provide you with a balanced diet for a one-year period. This is very important, since most of us are not professional dieticians. However, you will find that the dehydrated food programs usually do not contain any real meat, but instead, a meat substitute. The cost will vary, depending on the company that canned the dehydrated food. However, freeze-dried programs do contain real meat (*B).

In Appendix B, we will give a list of some food companies from which you can obtain quality dehydrated foods.

Dehydrate Your Own Food

If someone had asked me two years ago, between the basic methods of preserving food—canning, freezing, dehydrating—which one would retain the most nutrients, enzymes,

Preservation type and amount	gm. protein	mg. calcium	Total gm. carb. & fiber	mg. vit. C	mg. iron
100 gm. apricots					
canned in syrup	.6	11	.4	-4	0.3
dehydrated	5.6	86	.8	15	5.3
frozen, sweet	.7	10	.6	20	.9
100 gm. peaches					
canned in syrup	1.8	18	91.2	13	1.4
dehydrated	21.8	81	399.2	63	15.9
frozen, sweet	1.8	18	102.5	50	2.3
100 gm. peas					
canned	15	---	56	40	7.7
dehydrated	109	---	273	20	23.1
frozen	24	---	58	60	9.1
100 gm. carrots					
canned	2.7	---	113	2	3.2
dehydrated	3.8	---	367	15	27.2
frozen	29.9	---	115	4	4.9

Table 7.1

vitamins, and so forth, I would have said freezing. In actuality, that is not the case at all. Dehydration retains the most of these essential parts of the food, by far. Following is a table showing the comparison between these methods, which was discussed on the video entitled, *Dehydrating Made Easy* (*B). This video is an excellent tool, showing you how to dehydrate and giving recommendations on dehydrators.

If you have your own garden, I certainly would recommend dehydration as a method for preserving the majority of your excess garden output. If you do not have a garden, you can go to a farmers' market or even your own supermarket and buy extra fruits and vegetables when they are in season and are very cheap. For example, you would want to buy excess strawberries in the spring and excess apples in the fall, because those

Preservation type and amount	mg phosphate	I.U. vit. A.	mg. potassium	mg. ribr.	mg. niacin
100 gm. apricots					
canned in syrup	15	1,740	234	.03	0.4
dehydrated	139	14,100	1,260	.10	3.6
frozen, sweet	19	1,680	229	.04	1.0
100 gm. peaches					
canned in syrup	54	1,950	590	.11	2.5
dehydrated	685	22,680	22,680	.43	35.2
frozen, sweet	59	2,950	562	.18	.18
100 gm. peas					
canned	---	2,010	---	---	---
dehydrated	---	4,010	---	---	---
frozen	---	3,020	---	---	---
100 gm. carrots					
canned	---	45,360	---	---	---
dehydrated	---	453,600	---	---	---
frozen	---	49,200	---	---	---

Analysis charts, U.S. Department of Agriculture Research
Table 7.1

are the seasons in which those two fruits come into production and are the cheapest at the stores and fruit stands. The dehydrators recommended on the video, *Dehydrating Made Easy,* by my wife, Jeani McKeever, are listed in Appendix B.

Freeze-Dried Food

There is a far superior method of preserving and compacting food than dehydrating, and that is freeze-drying. It is a very different process than air-drying. In freeze-drying, much more of the moisture is removed than with dehydrating. The food is frozen, so that all of the water particles become ice. It is then exposed to heat, so that the ice (water) instantly evaporates. This leaves the pieces of meat (yes, real meat), vegetables and fruit saturated with holes, sort of like styrofoam. It is funny to see this thing that looks like styrofoam in the shape of a half of a pear. Fruit like pears are delicious eaten dry or you can soak a piece of dried pear in water and it turns back into a pear!

This is the type of storage food that we most highly recommend. Freeze-drying is usually used for real meats and many of the premixed meals. If one can afford it, one can go totally with freeze dried, or at least add a certain amount of freeze-dried foods to an air-dehydrated food storage program in order to provide some real meats and some interesting varieties. The number-one rated producer of freeze-dried food today is Alpine Aire Gourmet Reserves. Their year's supply of food contains real meat, as well as premade entrees such as Shrimp Newburg and Chicken Rotelle. They all taste great! They make both a "no-cook" and a "cooking required" year's supply. The address of a distributor is given in *B.

No Cook and MRE Foods

One thing to keep in mind in making your decision about what kinds of provisions you wish to make concerning food for an emergency situation is that, unless you have properly prepared, during the initial hours or days following certain types of emergencies, you may be without electricity or a method of cooking, at least initially. It could be extremely handy and beneficial to have stored at least some foods that do not require cooking.

We also tend to presume a lot, when it comes to considering such things. There is always a possibility that you may not be able to remain stationary, but you may have to be mobile to get to an area of greater safety. In such cases, some of the light-weight, "no cook" meals in pouches made for backpackers could be of great advantage. Some of these come ready-to-eat (MRE's, as discussed in Chapter 1), while others just require the addition of either hot or cold water (no cook meals). Some of the grains and beans are great for a more stable environment, but should relocating be necessary on short notice, or cooking facilities need to be reestablished following a disaster, this is where "no-cooking-required foods" can come into play and be a tremendous asset.

Additionally, in a fallout shelter, heat dissemination can be a problem, so the "no cook" or MRE foods would be especially good for that. As was discussed in Chapter 1 in conjunction with 72-hour kits, the MRE's come 12 meals to a case. Each meal has 1500-1800 calories and you can get by on two per day. Thus, a case would last two people for three days. They are also ideal for quick evacuation. You may wish to consider storing a two-week supply of these. See *B for more information of how to obtain these.

How to Store the Basic Foods

Wheat has been a basic storage food from almost the beginning of history. It was the staple in the Old Testament times, the Roman Empire, and early America. In fact, up until the last twenty-five or thirty years, those who wanted to store food for long periods of time could only turn to basic foods, such as wheat, rice, corn, honey and so on. Even today, with all of the high quality dehydrated foods that are available, this basic type of storage still is an excellent way to store foods.

Before going into the basics of this type of storage, let us look at the advantages and disadvantages. The major advantage is that you can do it yourself and save some money. Not only can you save money by packing the food yourself, but the ingredients are lower in cost than those of other programs. You will find that the cost per meal for a 2,600-calorie per day diet will run only 25 to 50 percent of that of any other program.

The major disadvantage is the very limited menu, both in variety and color, that can be offered if you store only the basic foods, and more time and labor required in preparing them. Also, there is a mental shock of switching from a regular diet to one that contains only four to eight ingredients. This change is especially hard for the very young and the old. That is why it is so important to be sure to use the foods you have stored in your everyday cooking. If you do so, you will learn to use the products correctly and with confidence, and your family will learn to like them.

WHEAT: If you are only using basic foods in your storage, you will need about 300 pounds of wheat or other grains per person per year. Another way to think of it is 1 pound a day per person, or 365 pounds for a year. Care should be taken to purchase number 1 or 2 hard red winter or hard white spring wheat. Number 1 is preferable, as it has a protein content of 12-16 percent and a moisture content of less than 9 percent. From a nutrient and a storage-life standpoint, it is worth paying a little more to get the best. If you cannot find good wheat by yourself, I would suggest that you contact the Mormon chapel in your area. They have been storing food for a long time and usually know where to get the best wheat for the best price. If you store wheat, you will also need some sort of flour mill for grinding.

Wheat is easy to store. Many people have different ideas, but I am giving the one that I have found to be the best. I have not known this method to fail, if done properly. For every 100 pounds of wheat, you will need three 5-gallon cans. I suggest screw top cans, if possible. Otherwise the pressure-fit lids work as well, but they are not as easy to open and reseal. You will also need dry ice, which you can get at an ice house, fire extinguisher shop or sometimes at an ice cream store. Using gloves to protect your hands from the extreme cold, crush the dry ice (or have the ice house cut it into 3-inch squares for you, if possible), and place two to three ounces in the bottom of each container. I have found that it is most convenient to do a maximum of three containers at a time. Immediately fill the containers with your wheat and lay the lids on the cans. *Do not tighten the lids even slightly at this point. Shake the cans every ten minutes; this helps the carbon dioxide, which is being given off as the dry ice melts, to push the oxygen up and out of the can. Wait about thirty minutes and then tighten the lids as much as you can.*

Check the cans again in about twenty minutes. If they have started to bulge, loosen the lids and let the excess gas out. This step is necessary if you used too much ice or tightened the lids too soon after putting in the wheat. If the containers are relatively clear, they could now be painted to block out light, marked with contents and date, and stored in a cool, dry place. The paint should be oil-based enamel. I have seen wheat that was stored this way for over twenty years not only make great bread, but sprout well.

RICE: You can store rice by using the same method as for wheat. Due to the fat content of the husk, however, you cannot store brown rice for long periods of time. Therefore, use a good-quality, fortified white rice for your long-term storage. Rice, oats, barley and rye can be stored for variety, or instead of wheat if you have a family member who is allergic to wheat.

BARLEY, DRIED CORN, MILLET, CORN MEAL, MACARONI, AND SUCH: All of these can be stored in the same manner as wheat, as explained above. Always try to get the best quality available.

SOYBEANS AND OTHER LEGUMES: Whole dry soybeans (and other varieties of beans) can be used for long-term storage and stored in the same manner as wheat. If basic foods are the majority of your food storage program, plan on 75 pounds per person per year. Soybeans can also be used as a milk source, as well as being a terrific source of protein (better than hamburger). Dried beans and lentils will keep indefinitely, if stored properly. They can be sprouted for maximum nutrition (as can the grains), which also reduces their cooking time. There are some twenty-five varieties of legumes, including soybeans, black-eyed peas and black beans.

TVP and TSP meat substitutes made from soybeans are also good storage items.

NOTE: If you do not wish to pack these grains and legumes yourself, there are places you can purchase them prepacked. One of the best is from Nitro-Pak (*B). After much research and evaluation, they came up with a unique solution to the "plastic bucket dilemma." Plastic breathes and allows toxic odors to permeate through the plastic and contact the food. Also, the plastic itself gives off a "plastic" odor which can affect the taste of the foods. One last drawback to storing grains in sealed plastic buckets is that light (one of the five deadly food enemies) can also enter the bucket walls and over time could affect the nutritional value of the food inside.

Nitro-Pak now offers a wide range of bulk storage grains and legumes that are double packed in a space-age, dual-layered inner foil liner. By using this inner liner, your grains will receive the finest protection possible for long-term storage. The foil liner acts as a vapor barrier equal to that of a glass jar and as a permanent light barrier. In addition, each sealed liner exceeds the conventional nitrogen-probe method used by most dealers and is vacuumed tight to remove the oxygen and then sealed tight in a pure inert nitrogen atmosphere. The final step is to seal each 6-gallon, heavy-duty plastic container with a tight-fitting, gasketed lid. This method of packing bulk grains is the latest state-of-the-art canning process available and it will add an extra layer of protection, plus ensure your foods the absolute longest shelf life and freshness possible.

POWDERED MILK: This is one of the hardest items to store. First you must decide which type to store:

1. **Nonfat, Instant:** Easy to mix, good tasting, longest storing due to low fat content. This is the type that I suggest. More expensive than nonfat regular.
2. **Nonfat, Noninstant:** Least expensive, hardest to mix. Be sure not to get a baker's type, if this is to be for drinking. Once mixed, it is good tasting. Higher fat content than instant.

3. **Whole Milk, Noninstant:** Most expensive, shortest storage life due to fat content, somewhat difficult to mix, excellent tasting.

At best, expect six months to two years storage for powdered milk that is not stored in a can with most of the oxygen removed. There is no way to do this yourself. Therefore, if you want long-term storage milk, you must go to one of the specially-packed milks from one of the dehydrated food companies.

For temporary storage of powdered milk, for up to two years, here is the best program that I have found. Place a heavy-duty plastic trash sack inside of a good quality 5-gallon plastic container with a tight fitting lid. Fill the bag with powered milk, twist the top of the bag to close it, and seal it with the supplied tie. On top of the closed bag, place a sack of rock salt about the size of your fist. *Be sure that this is not in contact with the milk.* The salt will absorb moisture and keep it from the milk. Put on the lid and seal the edge with heavy masking tape. Date the lid and store the container in the coolest, driest place around your home, preferably in a dark area. *Never store milk in the top of a garage or in the attic.* Check the milk every six to nine months, replacing the salt if necessary. If you find any milk caked or rancid smelling, it should be used only in cooking or for feeding animals. It will not be good for drinking. I have seen milk that was stored this way for four years that was still excellent. If you are using a basic foods storage program, you can plan for 60 pounds of powdered milk per person per year.

HINT: If you are having trouble getting your family to drink powdered nonfat milk, it may be that you are not preparing it correctly. Start rehydrating your milk eighteen to twenty-four hours early. Mix it very well and place it in the refrigerator until it is needed. Mix it again before you serve it.

Also, note that Nitro-Pak has an excellent powdered milk which is nitrogen packed and will store for eight plus years (*B).

HONEY: Honey is one of the easiest foods to store. The important criterion here is the amount of water in the honey.

If the water content is too high, the honey will not crystallize but will usually turn black and be useless. You may use any type of honey for storage—clover, alfalfa or other types readily available in your particular area. It does not have to be processed. However, I suggest that it be cleaned of most parts of comb and bees before storing. All you need to do is to pour the honey into a clean plastic container and seal it tightly. Depending on the moisture content, it will crystallize within one to three months. To use it, just heat the container in a tub of hot water to melt it. If you are using a basic foods storage program, 40 pounds of honey per person per year is a good amount to store.

SUGAR: If you prefer, 40 pounds of sugar can be stored instead of honey. I have found that the same method used for storing powdered milk works well. You do not have to check the sugar, unless it is stored in a moist area. *Be sure that the salt is not touching the sugar, but is on top of a closed sack.*

SALT: Salt can be stored in almost anything, but be sure that it is kept as dry as possible. Salt can lose savor if allowed to become too moist and hot. Ten pounds would provide a year's supply for one person.

A Low-Cost Food Storage Program

Perhaps you have considered storing some food, but you assumed that it was far too expensive and not something that you could afford to do. Although some more deluxe food storage programs can get fairly costly, food storage need not be so. Following is a simple food storage program, wherein expense is not an excuse, and it is the very cheapest if you buy these foods in bulk and package them yourself. I am quoting here from a portion of an article written on the subject by Jeani McKeever, entitled, *"Low-Cost Food Storage and How to Use It."* (See *B for information on how to obtain reprints of the entire article.)

Most Simple Food Storage Program 1:
One Month Supply For One Person

20 lb. dried corn
20 lb. wheat
10 lb. soybeans
1 lb. salt
7.5 grams ascorbic acid

The above will supply a month's worth of complete food for one person, based on 2500 calories a day for an average man. The only essential thing lacking with the corn, wheat and soybeans is Vitamin C (although the wheat can be sprouted for this). Just 25 cents worth of ascorbic acid will give you a two months' supply. Soybeans can also be used to produce a milk for infants. Other beans, such as black beans or pinto beans could be stored instead of or in combination with soybeans. A pound is overkill on the salt that you would need, but it does not hurt to have some extra.

The cost of the above program, as of March 1992, was just $10.65, which provides food for one person for an entire month! Certainly the average person in this country can afford that much to have one month's worth of FOOD INSURANCE. A year's supply (Program 2) would just be 12 x Program 1 above ($127.80, as of March, 1992).

These basic foods can be stored a long time (easily twenty years or longer), if stored properly....

With this food storage program, you would need to have a wheat mill of some type (either hand or electric) to grind the grains and legumes in order to make breads and certain other items....

Granted, these are basic survival foods, not gourmet meals, but it is an easy, low-cost way to begin to store a reliable, nutritious reserve to have on hand for emergencies. If you wish to supplement these basics with additional items for variety, you can always add on from this starting place, but at least you would know that you had a reserve of basic foodstuffs that could see you through many types of calamities.

Some basic preparations of this type can be considered your Food Insurance Policy. Obviously, the time to buy any insurance, for it to do any good, is before disaster strikes.

In the article, Jeani goes on to share easy but tasty ways to use these "Low-Cost Storage Foods," including a simple "Three-Grain Bread Recipe" and instructions on how to make a "Quick and Easy Blender Bread." Cost does not have to be a major factor preventing you from making some type of basic provision for emergencies in the area of food.

A Food Storage Video

Dr. Barbara Fair, a Master Gardener and Food and Nutrition expert, has produced an excellent video entitled, *Vital Food Storage* (*B). In it, she gets into some of the details of a food storage program and she deals with the subject for an entire hour, whereas we can devote only part of a chapter to it. If you are going to have a food storage program, you need to get this helpful video tape. It will be of tremendous aid to you in designing a food storage program that fits your family. There is also a helpful book entitled *Cooking with Home Storage*.

PROTECTING YOUR FOOD SUPPLY

In Chapter 6, I dealt more extensively with violence and defense against it, in a generalized way. In this section, I am primarily addressing Christians, because they are the ones who frequently ask me questions about protecting a food supply. Christians often ask these types of questions: "If I have a nice supply of food stored and an emergency or a time of famine occurs, what do I do if a bunch of people decide to come and take my food? Do I give it to them? Do I kill them? How far do I go in protecting my food supply?"

This is one of the most difficult questions that I have to address in this book. I will first give you the answer that obviously must be:

YOU MUST DO WHATEVER GOD TELLS YOU TO DO AT THE MOMENT.

You might be thinking, "James, that's a real cop out." In a way it may be, but in a very real way it is not. I believe that God might lead one Christian family to protect their food with all their might, even to the point of killing those who would attempt to steal it. I also believe that God would lead other Christians to give most or all of it away. (Remember, your confidence should not be in any food that you have stored, but in *God!)*

Let me share a few thoughts with you on both sides of this question. For those inclined to be more militant in their defense, there is ample Scriptural justification for this stance. For example, it would have been a sin for Aaron, in the Old Testament, to have learned to be a swordsman. God had called him to be a priest. On the other hand, it would have been a sin for Joshua not to have become one of the best swordsmen in the world. It is almost inconceivable to most of us that God would have commanded Joshua to go into a certain town and kill everyone in it, including the old people and the babies. But God actually commanded him to do that very thing at Jericho. In doing otherwise, Joshua would have been disobeying God.

Some Christians who tend to be pacifists think that if another Christian is learning karate, or taking shooting lessons, he is violent and out of touch with the will of God. We cannot know what God's will is for another. Each Christian must do what God leads him to do. I am perfectly convinced in my heart that God leads some Christians to learn these skills.

Another justification for "keeping what you have" is the parable of the ten virgins (Matthew 25:1-13). As you may remember, five virgins brought extra oil, and five did not. When the lamps of the five who did not have any extra oil went out, just about at the time the bridegroom was coming, they asked the five virgins who had extra oil for some of theirs and they were denied it. Those who had prepared did not give of their surplus to those who had not prepared. I think that, without violating any of the principles of the Scriptures, we could apply this to the food situation.

When Jesus sent out the seventy in Luke 10, He told them to not take anything with them—not a bag, not shoes, not a sword, nothing. However, in the upper room at the last supper, when He knew He was going to be leaving, He gave the disciples this command:

> **35 And He said to them, "When I sent you out without purse and bag and sandals, you did not lack anything, did you?" And they said, "No, nothing."**
>
> **36 And He said to them, "But now, let him who has a purse take it along, likewise also a bag, and let him who has no sword sell his robe and buy one...."**
>
> —Luke 22

Why did Jesus now tell them to buy a sword? In today's vernacular, it would be like telling them to buy a .45-caliber handgun. Did He expect them to buy the equivalent to a .45 and carry it with them and never use it? Obviously not. He would not tell them to sacrifice to buy something unless He wanted them to be prepared to use it.

On the other side of the question, we also see in the Scriptures that if a person is willing to give away his food—as was the boy with the fish and the loaves (John 6:1-14)—frequently God miraculously multiplies the food that is left. God could well lead Christians to give away all of their food so that their reliance would be totally on Him.

Those who would say that you should not defend your food supply would point to many of the teachings of Christ, such as going a second mile if a man compels you to go the first mile, and giving a man your coat also if he asked for your shirt (Matthew 5:39-41). Certainly sharing without resisting would seem to be in keeping with the spirit of Christ's teaching. This would surely be Scriptural justification for a Christian who felt that he should store up food but not defend it.

In short, I believe that, as a man stores up food for his family and himself, that food should be under God's control. God may lead him to give some of it or even all of it away, or He may lead him to keep it and defend it. Both are exemplified in the Scriptures. The key is obedience to the voice of God.

STORE WHAT YOU EAT
AND EAT WHAT YOU STORE

I would recommend that each family have stored at least a three-week supply of their regular wet pack food that they eat from day to day. If one has a nuclear fallout shelter, then I would recommend having fourteen days' worth of frozen food there, ideally food that does not require cooking, such as sandwiches, fried chicken, strawberries and other fruits, fish that has already been cooked, granola bars, and so forth.

However, in addition to that, it is wise for a family to have a one-year supply of food of some type stored up. Let me hasten to add that I have run across many people who have made a comment something like this: "Some years ago I bought a one-year supply of food for my family that was supposed to last for ten years and, after ten years, I hadn't needed it so I gave it away. Now I have nothing stored." That is not necessarily wise thinking. First of all, much of that food will still be edible, though lower in nutritional value after ten years. The companies simply guaranteed it to last for ten years, although items like the cans of wheat would last indefinitely. So, much of the food was given away that would still have been a good basis for a food storage program.

Second, their investment was an insurance policy. Just like your home, life or car insurance, you hope you will never need to use these policies, but it is comforting to know they are there. And it is wise to make these types of insurance provisions, in case you should need them.

However, the real, fundamental problem is that people like those I have just described bought a year's supply of food, stuck it in their garage and never even opened any of the boxes. If a time of emergency had come, they would have had to live off of that food that they were not accustomed to preparing or eating. Thus, they would have had an immediate total change of diet which upsets the physical system and could cause diarrhea, upset stomach and other problems. Believe me, in a time of emergency, you do *not* want to change your diet and start eating foods that you are not used to eating, if you have any choice in the matter.

If you do store a year's supply of dehydrated and freeze-dried food, here is what I would recommend. It should be used on an ongoing rotational basis, so that you always have a good, fresh supply. My recommended method for doing this is that one day each week you eat all three meals out of the food that you have stored. When one of the large cans eventually gets empty, you replace just that can. That way, every seven years, you will have completely eaten through your entire food storage supply and will have replaced it. This cycle would go on every seven years. You should be willing to do that. *You should regularly eat what you store.*

If you are not willing to eat out of your stored dehydrated food one day a week, then you should go to a food storage program that is completely composed of wet pack, freeze dried, no cook meals and frozen foods that you *will* eat. *It is important to date every can and every package with a permanent marking pen, so that you always use the oldest first.* But, you need to think through the fact that having a year's supply of wet pack and frozen foods might take quite a number of top-opening freezers and you must be able to provide electricity to them during times of emergency. And to store enough of those types of foods for a year probably would take ten times the cabinet space that you have in your kitchen. *You must keep using the food, rotating it, and restocking.* That way, you will learn which items you have stored that are not your favorites and you can replace them with something that you prefer.

Having a year's supply of food is obviously handy for emergencies. That emergency could even be that the bread-winner for your family is laid off or disabled from work for a year or two. In such a case, a stored supply of food could come in very handy.

It is also possible that famine could hit our planet on a worldwide basis. If you believe the Bible, it is noteworthy that it predicts a famine at the end of this age. If a famine does occur, some of that food you have stored could become more precious than gold.

FAMINE PREDICTED IN THE BIBLE

We do not know what will cause the famine that the Bible predicts will occur at the end of this age. Let us consider what the book of Revelation says about that coming famine:

5   And when He broke the third seal, I heard the third living creature saying, "Come." And I looked, and behold, a black horse; and he who sat on it had a pair of scales in his hand.

6   And I heard as it were a voice in the center of the four living creatures saying, "A quart of wheat for a denarius, and three quarts of barley for a denarius; and do not harm the oil and the wine."

—Revelation 6

A quart of wheat would feed a family for just one day and, in the time in which that passage was written, a denarius was a day's wage. So what it is telling us is that a time will come when the average working man will have to spend his full day's wage in order to buy enough food for his family and himself.

Being an economist, I would love to delve into the economic and social implications of this. Let it be sufficient to say that the result would be a total upheaval in our economic and social systems as we know them today. Frequently, out of such upheaval comes a dictator. Since it appears that food shortages are inevitable, we should examine various ways to prepare for these disasters. There are five basic strategies that I see employed by people around me today. These are:

1. Do nothing; trust "the system" to take care of you.
2. Have a food storage program.
3. Have a well-developed garden.
4. Have a greenhouse for food production.
5. Move to a farm.

Do Nothing—Trust the System
To Take Care of You

In my opinion, the man who adopts the "do nothing" strategy is violating some basic principles of God. The Bible says that if a man does not take care of his own family, he has denied the faith and is worse than an infidel:

8   But if anyone does not provide for his own, and especially for those of his household, he has denied the faith, and is worse than an unbeliever.

—1 Timothy 5

This verse tells us that a Christian who does not make preparation in order to be able to take care of his family in times of emergency is worse off than one who does not profess to be a Christian.   If a man makes no preparation for emergencies, he is as foolish as the five virgins who did not take extra oil with them when they went out to meet the bridegroom (Matthew 25:1-13). Here we are not talking about extra oil, but extra *food*.

In fact, I would suggest going further than preparing to provide just for your own family.   I believe it could be important for us to store up extra so that we could feed hungry friends, relatives and neighbors in a time of emergency.   It might be wise in looking at food storage to consider the possibility that you may indeed have an unexpected mouth or two that you might need to feed.

SUMMARY AND CONCLUSION

I first suggested going on a ten-day fast so that you can **know** that your body and your family can handle going without food for a period, if the need arises. In addition, the fast will have significant cleansing and detoxifying effects on your body and it could even cure some of your physical problems. One of the significant advantages of becoming familiar with fasting is that, if your family did have to go without food for a week, the children would not be wailing that they were hungry and your heart would not be torn in half in worry about them. The children need to be able to participate and realize that they too can fast for a period without dying.

Certainly fasting is not starvation, as some people will try to scare you into thinking. In the worst case, with an average, healthy individual, starvation would begin about forty days or more after you started fasting, *after* your body had used up all the stored energy and when it begins cannibalizing vital, necessary cells. At this point, an unmistakable, gnawing hunger would return, which is God's signal that you should definitely end your fast. I also pointed out that after a couple of days at the start of the fast, the hunger passes and you likely will not experience hunger again during the remainder of a ten-day fast. We have seen that we *can* fast, if necessary.

However, it is more desirable in times of emergency to be able to eat. Your handy grocery store could either not be accessible or it could be empty. Therefore, you need to consider having your own food storage program. Ideally, you would have a few weeks' worth of your regular food and, in addition to that, a mini-reserve of MRE meals and a one-year supply of dehydrated and freeze-dried foods. One day a week, it would be wise to eat out of the stored food that you have, so that every seven years, your supply would have been rotated and you would have a fresh supply.

STEP 7: *ACQUIRE AT LEAST A ONE-YEAR SUPPLY OF LONG-TERM STORAGE FOOD FOR EACH MEMBER OF YOUR FAMILY.*

In the consideration of having a reliable food supply, the aspects of moving to a farm, having a garden and a hydroponic greenhouse are subjects beyond the scope of this book, but they will be included in a forthcoming book in this *Preparation Series* entitled, *Preparation for Self-Reliant Living.*

What we are dealing with in this book is preparing for emergencies that could strike us at any time. I am sure that, like the Boy Scouts, you would rather "Be Prepared" than suffer the consequences of being unprepared or ill prepared for an emergency when it hits. The time to prepare is *now.*

Let us now take a look at earthquakes in particular. You may think that your area is not in any danger of an earthquake, but according to FEMA (the Federal Emergency Management Agency), forty-five out of the fifty states are at risk of a severe earthquake. Let us see if there are some simple things you can do for the safety of your family.

Chapter 8

SPECIAL PREPARATION FOR EARTHQUAKES

Many areas of our country are susceptible to earthquakes. The potential areas are not limited just to southern California, but they range across the nation to Missouri, New England and down to the Carolinas. As we mentioned earlier, forty-five out of fifty states are at risk according to the Federal Emergency Management Agency (FEMA). Actually, an earthquake could occur anywhere on the planet at any time.

Since the potentiality of an earthquake is such a widespread danger, and one can happen without any warning (at least with hurricanes there is a little warning time), I felt it was important to give a few words on special considerations of preparation for an earthquake.

SAFETY DURING
THE ACTUAL EARTHQUAKE

The big danger during an earthquake is from falling objects. Most deaths and injuries result from objects that fall and crush or maim an individual, or from flying glass that can cut severely. The ideal place to be when an earthquake hits is in a flat, treeless meadow. Ground ruptures are seldom the cause of casualties. Most of the hazards are manmade. It is best not to be under signs or poles that can snap, or near tall buildings or under bridges that can collapse. Neither is it safe to be on the lower side of reservoirs and storage tanks, as they can rupture and spill their contents.

If you are inside a house or building when an earthquake hits, *stay inside.* It is best to move quickly to a position in a doorway, in a bathroom, in a corner or under a table. The reason for choosing these areas is that they have extra structural reinforcement and will tend to hold up ceilings and roofs, preventing them from collapsing on you. It is also wise to grab a coat or blanket, if possible, to put over your head to avoid facial cuts from flying glass.

If you are outside, *stay outside.* Many accidents and injuries during earthquakes occur when people are leaving or entering buildings. You should try to get out from under things that could fall on you—telephone and electrical poles, trees and the like. Since the walls of buildings can fall outward during an earthquake, it is best to move to as open an area as possible. It is likely that, during the earthquake, electrical wires will be snapped and fall. Of course, at all cost, you should avoid these falling electrical wires.

Once the shaking has stopped, there will be time to evaluate your position and plan what actions to take. It is very likely that there will be fires to be extinguished (created from broken gas lines). When a quake hits, any or all of the following could occur:

1. The power may go off.
2. Water supplies may dribble dry.
3. Phones may be dead or tied up.
4. Sewer and gas lines may be broken.
5. Roads and freeways may be blocked by collapsed bridges, landslides, downed power lines, debris and stalled vehicles.
6. Fires may break out, and there could be no water with which to put them out.
7. Police and fire services may not be available to help you.
8. The bottled goods in drugstores and grocery stores could all be smashed and unusable.

HOME SAFETY PREPARATION
FOR EARTHQUAKES

I was in Guatemala in 1976 between the two big earthquakes. My wife and I were there again a few months later and talked with people who had experienced the quake. The universal comment was that the noise was so deafening that it sounded like they were in the middle of a battlefield. Can you imagine the sound for blocks around as everyone's bookcases were tumbling over dumping out books, tall China cabinets were falling over, breaking all of the dishes in them, grandfather clocks were crashing over, wall units were falling and spilling their contents, and food and dishes were flying out of the cupboards? The quake happened at night in Guatemala. After it was over, people went into their living rooms and kitchens to find books, broken mirrors and dishes, and other items strewn everywhere.

This brings us to one of the first things that we can do in preparing our homes for an earthquake. We can put screw eyes in the back of tall pieces of furniture, and eye screws in the studs in the walls behind them, and wire them to the walls so that the furniture will not topple over. One of the worst potentials for a household accident from an earthquake is the hot water heater. During the 1971 California earthquake, a friend's hot water heater "walked" from one side of the garage to the other, obviously breaking the gas pipe and water pipes that connected it. A hot water heater is already top-heavy and unstable, and it is usually a prime victim of earthquakes. The diagram in Figure 8.1 shows how this might be cabled to the wall.

In addition, in an earthquake, drawers can fly open and spill their contents. Positive action drawers, such as are found in most boats, would be very nice to have in a home that is in a prime earthquake zone. Since dishes will tend to fall out of cupboards, a child-guard latch or a screen-door-type hook could be placed on the outside of each cupboard in the kitchen, and latched when not in use. Heavy, hanging mirrors and things of this nature will tend to come off of their hooks and crash to the floor during an earthquake. Anything that is tall and heavy

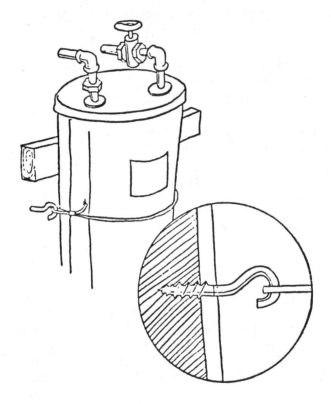

Figure 8.1

especially if it is near your bed, should be properly secured to the wall.

Imagine what it would be like if the Jolly Green Giant were to grab your home on each side and shake it vigorously. If you make a complete check of your home with this in mind, undoubtedly you will be able to discover things that you could easily take care of in a preventative way. The way to prevent damage to your property and harm to your family is to take a little time to provide precautionary measures.

Once the quake is over, if you are unhurt, your priorities should be:

1. To keep from getting hurt.
2. To help as best you can those who are injured.
3. To prevent further injuries and property damage.

If medical help is unavailable, do all that you can to aid, comfort and reassure those who are hurt or frightened. Do not move injured people unless they are in immediate danger of further injury. As we mentioned in an earlier chapter, along with providing first aid, you should put out any fires as a top priority. However, even before you put out the fires, you should turn off the gas line coming into the house. As was mentioned earlier, there is a special combination tool available that is designed for turning off both gas and water (*B).

After you have extinguished any fires, then turn off the water coming into the house. After you have taken care of all these needs in your own home, you can go out on a patrol of your neighborhood to help other people in need. Move cautiously and wear protective shoes. Be constantly alert for hazards that could be magnified by aftershocks.

Even a tiny spark from an electric wall switch, cigarette or flame can ignite accumulated gas. Of course, should you suspect that there are damaged lines or possible gas leaks, immediately turn off the gas main and ventilate the area. *Indoor candles and open flames, such as matches and cigarette lighters, are earthquake "no-no's."* Aftershocks may cause gas leaks, or even tip over your unattended candles. If the fire department cannot reach you, the smallest flame, unchecked, can touch off a neighborhood holocaust. As far as extinguishing flames, the best thing is proper fire extinguishers, but wet towels can be used and reused to beat out small fires, extending precious water supplies. Shoveled dirt, potted plants, and even potato salad can be used to snuff out flames that could destroy a house.

Fallen electrical wires can be a real hazard, as we have mentioned. To rescue someone from wires is to seriously risk your life. A wrong move can kill you. If you attempt such a rescue, you must stand on dry, nonmetallic surfaces (ground, paper, or rubber matting, and such), remaining totally and continually insulated from both the victim and the wires. The victim and the wires must be separated, by pushing or pulling them apart, using only bone-dry, nonmetallic, nonconducting objects (broomsticks, long boards, plastic pipe, and so forth).

Do not waste food. First use food out of your refrigerator. After this is used up, begin to utilize the frozen food out of your freezer. Even if the electricity has been turned off, your freezer still may preserve the food for several days. (Top-opening freezers are best for this.) If you purchased a small electrical generator to run your necessary utilities, of course the food could stay frozen for weeks.

Makeshift toilets must be kept thoroughly disinfected and tightly covered. Their contents should be buried deep or kept in sealed plastic bags or trash containers, along with other garbage and refuse. Keep refuse away from hungry and homeless animals that might gather around it.

Keep your transistor radio tuned in for broadcasts of conditions and emergency recommendations.

There is a real danger of an aftershock or second earthquake that can be as bad as the first. Frequently, the first big aftershock will create more damage than the initial quake, since many of the structures that have been weakened by the first shaking will topple with the second. It has been my experience that less severe aftershocks frequently will continue for many days after the first one or two big quake movements.

TAKE THE TIME TO PREPARE

For about $50, you can make a home fairly safe from earthquakes. A few eye screws and pieces of wire and cable can be used to attach tall furniture and the water heater to the walls behind them, as we discussed earlier. Installing hooks on cupboards, and purchasing some water storage barrels (less than $20) and a porta-potty could make your survival, and that of your family, much easier during and immediately following an earthquake. All it takes to make these preparations is a very little bit of money and a little time.

There are three books that I have found helpful with regard to details about how to prepare for an earthquake. The first two are smaller—almost booklets—and the third one is an extensive volume which even gets into construction considerations for making new buildings more earthquake proof. If you are interested in pursuing the subject, I trust that you will find these books useful:

The Earthquake Handbook
By Chuck Coyne

Earthquake Home Preparedness
By Ruth Brent

Peace of Mind in Earthquake Country
By Peter Yaney

SUMMARY AND CONCLUSION

This conclusion will be short and sweet. Since earthquakes can happen anywhere, it is wise to make simple preparations for an earthquake, regardless of where you live. Strapping a hot water heater to the wall is something that requires little effort and almost no expense. Other items mentioned in the early chapters of this book should also be done in preparation for an earthquake. Building your own customized first aid and medical boxes and storing adequate drinking water are two of the essentials that we have already discussed.

STEP 8:   EDUCATE YOUR HOUSEHOLD IN EARTHQUAKE PRECAUTIONS AND SECURE HOT WATER HEATER, TALL FURNITURE AND CUPBOARDS.

Now we need to look at a very interesting subject. After a disaster, if there is no electricity, most credit card machines would not work and the inside teller machines at the bank would be dead, as well at the ATM's. This means that you would not be able to buy things with credit cards or checks. What would you use? See the next chapter for the answer.

Chapter 9

BEG, BARTER, BUY OR STEAL

It is possible that, after an emergency occurs, no matter how good your preparations have been, there may be some things you need that you did not store ahead of time. If these are essential items, then you are going to need to be able to acquire these, one way or the other. Since my Christian heritage says that stealing is wrong, I do not recommend stealing. That leaves you with three choices: beg, barter or buy.

BUYING THE ITEMS YOU NEED

You would like to be able to buy the goods or the services that you lack, especially right after an emergency is over. However, after many emergencies, people will not accept checks. With no electricity, ATM's will not work and credit cards cannot be verified. It is conceivable that, after a very major disaster, merchants would not be willing to take credit cards. Therefore, the ideal would be to be able to buy the items that you need with cash or goods.

My recommendation is that you have from one to three months' worth of your net salary in cash, in the currency of your country. This is the most easily recognized and accepted method of making financial transactions in times after an emergency. There are some problems with this, but the advantages far outweigh the problems. Let's see if we can solve some of those problems.

You might ask, "If I have that much cash at home, couldn't someone steal it?" That is a good question. Remember the old adage that:

A thief cannot steal what he cannot find.

One lady I know of put her cash in an old Tide box under her sink. A robber broke into their home and took some jewels and other things, but have you ever heard of a thief taking a box of Tide? Others have put cash in an empty paint can out in the garage where other full or partially-full cans of paint were stored. Fire could burn up the currency, so a small, fire-safe file could also be a good investment. You don't need a book or an expert to help you think of a place to put your cash where a thief would not find it; you just need to give the matter a little creative thought.

Another problem is that cash will depreciate with inflation. This is true, and there is nothing you can do about that. However, what you can do is to keep your reserve up with inflation. For example, if you put away $1,000 cash as your "emergency reserve," and inflation was 10 percent that year, at the end of the year, you could simply add $100 to the $1,000, so that your cash reserve would have the same purchasing power at the end of the year as it did at the beginning.

Another alternative would be to keep the cash in a safe deposit box at the bank, instead of keeping it in your home. During the 1933 bank crisis, when bank windows were closed, people could still get to their safe deposit boxes. However, if one of the signers of the safe deposit box dies, that box cannot be opened. Therefore, if you go the safe-deposit-box route, it would be better to put it in the name of a company or a trust.

So you can see that most of the problems with keeping a supply of cash on hand can be overcome. One-to-three month's worth of your net salary in cash could prove to be a very valuable provision immediately after an emergency, so that you can buy needed items or services. This could also come in handy in the event of a job loss or temporary disability.

STORING GOLD AND SILVER COINS

There are some writers who envisage the currency becoming worthless and people doing all of their purchasing at the grocery stores with the old silver coins or with gold coins. Whether or not they realize it, those who say this are implying that at that point in time, the U.S. government would be nonexistent and total anarchy would prevail because, if the U.S. government were still in existence, it would have the ability to enforce the use of our currency. If we are under a situation of total anarchy, we will have far bigger problems than buying a loaf of bread with a silver quarter.

Does this mean that I am against storing gold and silver coins? No, it does not. However, I would lean more toward storing gold coins than silver coins. Gold has traditionally been a store of value through the centuries. The price of gold in 1992 was substantially higher than that in 1972. Yet, the price of silver in 1992 was essentially the same as it was in 1972. You need to store something that will at least keep up with inflation and hopefully go up faster than inflation. Therefore, I recommend U.S. gold coins. If gold coins are too expensive for you, some silver coins could be accumulated to later exchange for gold coins when you accumulate enough.

WITH WHAT DO WE BARTER?

Let's just say that the emergency or disaster proves to be a gigantic one that is going to last for months or years, to the point that any cash or stored gold coins we may have had will have run out. What do we barter (trade) to other people in order to obtain the things that we want or need? If potential bartering is part of your envisioned future, then you will want to store up something with which to barter. Barter items should have several characteristics:

1. Something desired by almost everyone.
2. Something easily stored.
3. Something easily divisible into small units.

It may be that a great many things come to your mind, but just let me mention a few possibilities to probe your thinking:

NAILS: After almost every disaster, rebuilding is required, and nails will be in demand. You could store several of the large 50-pound boxes of nails of various sizes and barter these a handful at a time.

BOTTLES OF WINE: You could store extra bottles of wine or some other liquid that you think will be in high demand and could barter it a bottle at a time.

BULLETS: After a major long-lasting disaster, bullets could be in high demand. You could lay in a few cases of the most popular caliber bullets, such as .22, .223, .308, .45, 9mm and so forth, as potential barter items.

CONDOMS: In a very long-lasting major disaster, birth control pills may not be available and condoms could be in very high demand. (Keep in mind that condoms have a recommended shelf life of five years and your supply would need to be kept fresh.)

TOILET TISSUE, SOAP AND SHAMPOO: These are basic items that would always be in demand.

BATTERIES: If kept in a freezer, the shelf life of batteries is indefinite.

WHEAT: It could be that wheat, or some other whole grain that could be stored in 5-gallon buckets, could be bartered off for various items that you need.

Let me remind you that the consideration of bartering makes almost the same assumption as storing silver coins—that there won't be a U.S. government or any acceptable money and that things will be in total anarchy for months or years. I personally don't envisage that as a likely future scenario for the population as a whole. A stronger possibility is the debasement of the U.S. dollar, which means high inflation. Under that scenario, things that you store will have been purchased at a very cheap price.

The Bible points to a day when Christians who refuse the mark of the beast will not be able to buy or sell. In that eventuality, bartering will be the only way for them to acquire things.

Storing up some barter items, along with the other preparations, could prove to be wise, in any case.

TAKE CARE OF EACH OTHER

Begging is going to be a poor way to survive in emergency and disaster conditions. As long as the federal government is able, they will likely try to help you, but there could possibly be a point at which you would be on your own to take care of yourself, without any government aid.

You will fare far better if you are a part of a close-knit group from your church or synagogue, or some other such group, who are committed to each other and willing to share things with each other. By pooling your resources and talents, you will be able to survive and live much better than if you try to make it on your own. In preparing for emergencies, far too many people have the philosophy that it is "me against the world." Sitting at the mouth of a cave with some dehydrated food, some gold coins and a shotgun, daring anyone to come near, is not a life I would like to live. We are going to need each other. We are going to need community, and any preparation for a long-lasting disaster or emergency should include others, whether in your neighborhood or those with a common religious belief or philosophy about the future.

SUMMARY AND CONCLUSION

It is very likely that, regardless of how well thought out your preparations are, you will find that you still lack something, once a real emergency or disaster occurs. If you find yourself in that condition, you will have four choices of how you are going to acquire the needed goods and services:

1. Beg
2. Barter (trade)
3. Buy
4. Steal

Since I am against stealing, and begging is not very appealing or commendable, that leaves us the choice of making some preparation either to be able to *buy or barter* for those goods and services.

This is the ninth major item in our preparation for emergencies, given in approximate order of priority in this book.

STEP 9: LAY ASIDE THREE MONTHS' WORTH OF CASH. IN ADDITION, CONSIDER STORING GOLD COINS OR BARTER ITEMS.

Now where do you go to sleep and eat? If your house has been flattened by a tornado, hurricane, earthquake, nuclear explosion, volcanic explosion or some other event, you will need someplace to go where you can sleep and eat that is safe and will provide you with protection.

Chapter 10

SHELTER—
"THE HAPPY ROOM"

As we approach this next very important subject of providing shelter, there are many titles this chapter could have, which would be names for an emergency shelter. Some such names might be:

> The Storm Cellar
> The Root Cellar
> The Fallout Shelter
> The Fun Room
or
> The Happy Room

First I will set out methods for providing temporary shelter. Then we will look at methods for building a permanent shelter for emergencies, and my preferred approach—that of "the Happy Room."

THE OLD STORM CELLAR

I mentioned in Chapter 1 that I grew up in near Dallas, Texas, which is part of what is called "tornado alley." The destruction left by a tornado can be incredible. As I said earlier, nearly all of my relatives living around the Dallas area had a "storm cellar" where they could go in case a tornado was going to hit. These were usually very simply constructed. They dug a ditch about 8 feet wide, 8 feet deep and 10 feet or more long. They put some heavy planks across the ditch and then covered it back up with the dirt they had dug out, which left a mound about 4 or 5 feet high. The door down to the storm cellar was almost horizontal—probably about 15 degrees from horizontal—and it had earthen steps down into it.

These storm cellars were always a very cool place and I used to love to go down into them. The women of the house usually put jars of foods they had canned on shelves in the storm cellar. There were also a few chairs, a couple of cots and things of this nature. These were designed to protect people against tornados which last, at most, just a few minutes. They were not intended to be occupied for long periods of time.

Also in the storm cellar, people commonly kept root vegetables in bins (carrots, potatoes, turnips, and so forth), so sometimes it was called a *root cellar* instead of a *storm cellar*. Of course, back in those days, we did not have nuclear devices, but today it could also be used as a *fallout* shelter to protect one from the radioactivity of nuclear fallout.

Today, with much more sophistication, tools and techniques, and knowing that we may have to occupy such a shelter for up to two weeks in the event of nuclear fallout, the root cellar would most likely be constructed of cement block, poured concrete or prestressed concrete. It would also be desirable for it to have lights, ventilation and a toilet. It could also be of the cylinder-type made out of old fuel tanks.

If someone were farsighted enough to have a root cellar stocked with a month's or a year's supply of food and enough stored water to last for two weeks, that person or family could survive many disasters. The minimum amount of water you would want to have for a family of four for two weeks would be 56 gallons, in order to have enough water for drinking, cooking, brushing your teeth and washing your fingers up to the first knuckle. However, I recommend 120 gallons. If water is needed for longer than two weeks, then purification supplies should be stored.

As I said in Chapter 1, if someone had had a well-supplied storm cellar in the southern tip of Florida during Hurricane Andrew or in Hawaii during Hurricane Iniki in 1992, life certainly would have been much easier for that family.

One thing that is peculiar about southern Florida is the high water table. To have an underground storm cellar (root cellar, fallout shelter) there would require having a sump pump to eliminate any encroachment of subsurface water. However, this is not an unusual thing. Many basements in the northern part of our country have sump pumps to get rid of any excess moisture. A standby manual pump could be considered in case there were no electricity.

Let's say that someone in southern Florida had a well-stocked storm cellar. When the orders to evacuate the area came, they could have gone into their storm cellar instead, and they would have been right there at their home. In fact, they could have remained in their home almost until the last minute and then simply gone into their storm cellar. As soon as the hurricane winds passed, which only lasted minutes (not hours), they immediately could have come back up to put out any fires that may have started from broken gas pipes or downed electrical wires. In general, they would have been the first who could have taken care of their property, while others were many, many miles away from their homes. With a regular radio and a CB radio installed in their storm cellar, they could have been in contact with what was going on.

If the roof of their home had been slightly damaged, they first could have repaired the roof so that any rains would not damage the furniture and other things that remained in the home. (For this and other reasons, I recommend having a roll of heavy mil, clear plastic sheeting which is available at most home improvement stores.) The people who were able to stay in a storm cellar right on their own property could also have guarded it from the many looters that came into the area of destruction. In general, they would have been far better off than a family that had to flee 100 or 200 miles from their home and rely on the government or someone else to feed and shelter them and provide them with water.

Almost any home owner could build a storm cellar in his or her backyard. It may be one of the old types with a dirt floor and dirt walls. In times past, they have been very effective in protecting from tornados, hurricanes and cyclones and they would still be effective today. There is rarely a backyard in which you could not dig an 8 x 12-foot ditch, 8 feet deep, and put boards over it and cover it back up. The expense would be very little, particularly if you did the digging yourself and made it a fun family project. Bringing in a backhoe to dig the hole would be another possibility. Of course, there would be a cost factor to weigh for the backhoe, and it might bring attention to the fact that you have a storm cellar, but it could be done and it is another option to consider.

As I mentioned earlier, a storm cellar is a cool place that could be used to store bulk food and root vegetables. This is why these types of cellars were also commonly called root cellars. Ideally, you would not simply have this place only to be used the event of a storm; you would also like to be able to make regular use of it.

We are also going to look at using the storm cellar as a fallout shelter to protect one from gamma rays that are emitted from the particles of nuclear fallout. Even if you think the likelihood of a nuclear encounter is very small, I would encourage you to continue reading this section for basic knowledge, if nothing else. There are excellent ideas about fallout shelters that you probably would want to include in a storm cellar.

UNDERSTANDING NUCLEAR FALLOUT

You may think that a likelihood of a major nuclear war is very low and, of course, that is your prerogative. However, I would encourage you to reconsider that position. As of 1992, Russia was still building one Trident attack submarine every thirty-three days at a cost of $1 billion each. Why were they still building these, especially when their economy was in shambles? When some well-meaning western government loaned Russia $5 billion, essentially that translated into three new attack submarines (even if that was not what the western government intended the money be used for). Basically, those funds did not go to the people. There has never been a military machine such as that built by the Soviet Union (now Russia and its Commonwealth of Affiliated Countries) that has not been used at some point. The Russian bear has not become a pussycat. The possibility of a nuclear war is still something that one should consider seriously when preparing for emergencies.

The Bible says "My people are destroyed for lack of knowledge..." (Hosea 4:6). It is certainly true that a lack of knowledge concerning a nuclear encounter and nuclear fallout could cause many to perish. If the dust from a nuclear explosion were to cover a can of corn and it received gamma radiation, the corn in the can would not be radioactive at all, and it would still be very edible. Of course, you would want to wash off the can before opening it. The gamma rays passing through it would be much like x-raying a can of corn. After being x-rayed, it is still edible corn. Many people would starve to death, while having very edible food in their cupboards, because they thought the food had become radioactive.

There are many other misconceptions concerning nuclear explosions, so we need to start at the very beginning.

The Two Phases Of A Nuclear Explosion

If there is nuclear war, it is possible that a nuclear bomb (or bombs) could be exploded near where you live or work.

I have found that there are two distinct phases involved in a nuclear explosion, and different actions are required in each of the phases. The first phase is the initial blast wherein you have the thermal waves, the initial radiation and the wall of fire. During the second phase, the materials that were blown to fine bits in the initial explosion (earth, trees, buildings, and such), which have become miniature transmitters of radiation (alpha, beta and gamma particles) and have been lifted 70,000 to 120,000 feet, gradually float back to the earth. This is the "fallout" of the nuclear cloud of radioactive dust that was created.

The Initial Blast

It is possible that there would be some warning of a nuclear attack. If this is so, in the U.S. the warning sirens would sound a steady tone for about three to five minutes and when they started warbling, that would mean *take cover*. For detailed information at that time, you should tune to any AM or FM radios in your area for emergency information.

However, let's assume the worst case, where there is no prior warning. The first thing you would notice would be a very bright flash (*do not* look at the light) and, likely, an earthquake-type tremor. Within a very few seconds, you would get the blast wave and also the thermal and radiation impact. One thing to note is that this wave travels in a straight line. It does not go around corners. If there were a large rock between you and the blast, this wave would go over your head, if you were to sit in the "shadow" of the rock. At first, the blast wave will move outward from the nuclear explosion and then, almost like the tide, come back into the vacuum that was left from the explosion.

All is not total destruction in a nuclear blast. There is a central area, of course, that will be totally annihilated. However, it is interesting to note that in the Hiroshima blast, the Hiroshima Electric Building was just 1 mile from ground zero and was basically undamaged.

This brings us to what you should do in the event of such an explosion. If you see a nuclear flash, you should immediately *dive for cover*. When the blast hits, it will shatter windows. There will be thousands of needle-like fragments of glass flying at very high speed. If you are at an office, crouch behind your desk so that the desk is between you and the blast. If you are outside, dive for a ditch or lay down behind a log and shield your eyes and face. If you are at home, dive under a coffee table or bed. One of the main things to do is to get away from windows because of the glass, radiation and heat that will be coming through them. The closer you are to the explosion, the less time there will be between the flash and the blast wave. Even at 30 miles, you probably only have about 20 or 30 seconds. This means that you are going to have to move, and move *fast*.

It is likely in a nuclear attack that two missiles would be sent to each target, which means that possibly a second explosion is coming. Therefore, once you take cover, remain there for at least two minutes. Do not try to run to another room or change position until both the outward surge and the inward surge of the blast have occurred, and you are pretty sure that there is not going to be a second explosion. Then you should have time to do a number of things, such as put out fires and move to a shelter. Depending on your situation and the wind conditions, the fallout will probably not occur for twenty minutes to eight hours. Only a tiny percent of the people will be killed in the initial blast. The vast majority of the deaths will occur because of the subsequent fallout. That is the real danger, and the one from which you must protect yourself. Before looking at *how* to protect yourself from fallout, let us first examine exactly what it is.

Radioactive Fallout

Tiny particles of material are rapidly carried upward in the great boiling mushroom cloud by the intense heat and upward air currents created by the fireball. When the particles are at 70,000 to 120,000 feet, the heat in the air currents will have largely dissipated. This radioactive "cloud" is then caught up in the prevailing winds of the stratosphere, and is carried away from the point of detonation. The particles of debris begin gradually to sink back towards the earth, since they no longer have the heated air to support them. They "fall out" of the nuclear cloud toward the ground below. These particles range in size from coarse grain sand down to a very fine powder. The larger particles resemble grit or dust, while the smaller ones look like fine ashes.

Each of the particles emits three types of rays—alpha, beta, and gamma. The alpha rays can only travel through 1 inch of air. The beta particles can travel through 10 feet of air, but the gamma rays are capable of traveling half a mile through air and can penetrate considerable thicknesses of solid material with ease.

These particles are like microscopic bullets. When they pass through your body, they actually do internal damage. If you get enough of them passing through in a short period of time, your body's natural healing processes cannot work fast enough to heal you, and you will die. On the other hand, you can take the same amount of particles over a longer period of time and your body will be able to repair itself and recover from the damage. Because of the extremely short range of the alpha and beta particles, you do not have to worry about them, unless you actually get fallout on your person (clothes, skin or hair). Assuming that you take care to prevent this, the major danger then is from the gamma radiation. Remember that the gamma rays travel in straight lines and are stopped by approximately 2½ feet of dirt or 18 inches of concrete. If you had a pile of gamma-producing radioactive material in one place, and a large pile of dirt between you and it, you could sit safely behind the dirt. The rays would pass over your head and around you.

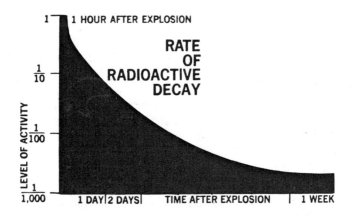

Figure 10.1

Another important thing to know is the rapid rate of the radioactive decay. Three or four days after an explosion, the radioactivity transmission from the particles is only about 1/100 of the level that it was at the time the bomb was exploded. Figure 10.1 shows this rapid decay rate.

It is very important to understand the measurement of this radiation. The basic measurement is the roentgen. This is sometimes referred to as REM (roentgen equivalent man). Frequently, in tables or graphs, it will be shown as "R" for an abbreviation. Table 10.1 (from *Scientific American*, November, 1976) shows the dosage it would take over a one-week period

compared to a one-month period in order to have the effects
that are listed.

Table 10.1

DOSE (IN REMS)		EFFECT
IF DELIVERED OVER ONE WEEK	IF DELIVERED OVER ONE MONTH	
150	200	THRESHOLD FOR RADIATION ILLNESS
250	350	5 PERCENT MAY DIE
450	600	50 PERCENT MAY DIE

Figure 10.2 shows the number of roentgens per hour that
you would receive standing in an open field at various distances
from the point of the explosion. As can be seen, the winds
carry the radioactivity only in one direction. This shows that
if you were 200 miles from a blast, even downwind, you would
have about eighteen hours to prepare before the fallout began.

A HYPOTHETICAL ATTACK

From pages 96-70 of *Survival Handbook,* we quote:

The hypothetical attack consisted of a total of 1,446 megatons
of nuclear weapons yield delivery to 224 targets in the United
States in the form of 263 bombs of 1, 2, 3, 8, and 10-megaton
yield. Targets included 70 metropolitan areas of importance in
terms of population, communications, industry, military bases,
and Atomic Energy Commission installations. All the bombs
were ground burst. The pattern of fallout from these hypothetical weapons bursts is shown on the maps. The fallout
distribution is shown as it would be at two different times after
the initial attack, illustrating the manner in which fallout spreads
with the prevailing wind, covering tremendous areas of the
country.

—The MacMillan Co., New York

DOSE RATE CONTOURS FROM FALLOUT AT 1, 6, AND 18 HOURS AFTER A SURFACE BURST WITH FISSION YIELD IN THE MEGATON RANGE (15 MPH EFFECTIVE WIND).

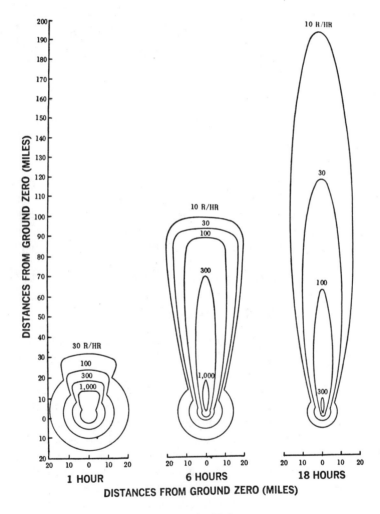

Figure 10.2

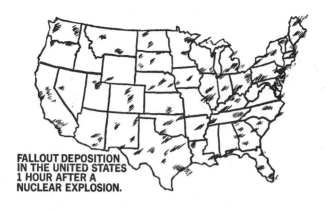

FALLOUT DEPOSITION
IN THE UNITED STATES
1 HOUR AFTER A
NUCLEAR EXPLOSION.

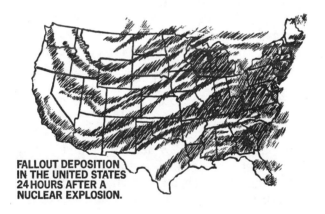

FALLOUT DEPOSITION
IN THE UNITED STATES
24 HOURS AFTER A
NUCLEAR EXPLOSION.

Figure 10.3

Wherever the nuclear bombs fall, the fallout will be downwind of the explosion. Most of it will land on the ground, and some on the roofs of buildings and houses. It is very important to know when the fallout is actually beginning, so that you can take shelter. One easy way to do this is to place clean plates (preferably of a solid pastel color) outside on each side of your house. These can be checked periodically; you will actually be able to see the fallout land on them. Once this begins to occur, it is time to take shelter.

SHELTERS TO SHIELD
AGAINST RADIATION

The first question that comes to mind in regard to shelters is, what about public shelters of the Civil Defense? In checking these, I found them to be totally inadequate. The metal water containers are empty, so that they will not rust. The cereal-based crackers stored there are quite old, and in many cases would cause you to be sick if you ate them. You are expected to bring your own bedding and flashlights to these public shelters. Even if they were in top-notch shape and completely stocked, living in a shelter like that from four to forty days could be quite a messy situation. You could have all sorts of sociological problems—everything from people panicking to somebody, who has snuck a gun into the situation, setting himself up as a miniature dictator.

Therefore, you should probably consider your own family fallout shelter. My recommendation is that you do not attempt to design one, but that you use professionally-designed fallout shelters. If you do decide to do it on your own, there are a number of things of which you should be aware. To shield yourself from the gamma rays, you would need one of the following: approximately 2½ feet of earth, 18 inches of concrete, 3½ feet of water or 6 feet of wood. The ideal, of course, is to have a shelter underground in your backyard or built in your basement. It should have a minimum of 10 square feet per person, although an 8- by 12-foot shelter is usually recommended for a family of four. Figure 10.4 shows a house with a basement before and after protection is installed for fallout. It includes things to do between the time of the blast and the time when fallout begins.

You will note that the corner of the basement where there are no vents was chosen for the shelter, and that a water bed was placed on top of the shelter, both for washing and additional protection. On the floor above the shelter, books (and anything with mass) were placed to absorb additional radiation. The shelter has a venting system with a hand crank, which is necessary because there may not be electricity. The air in the shelter will become stale when it is occupied;

therefore, the occupants will have to take turns cranking the ventilator fan. The air intake of the vent should be filtered. The door has a 6- by 6-inch slidable opening to view outside and to hold out your radiation rate measuring device.

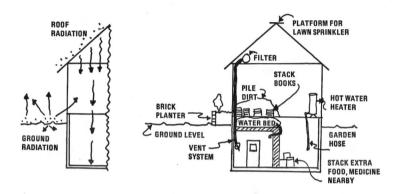

Figure 10.4

Shown in Figure 10.5 are some typical family shelters from *Survival Handbook*.

If a blast were to occur and no shelter has been provided, unless you were extremely near the blast, there would be time between the blast and the fallout to construct a makeshift shelter. If you were in a home with a basement, you should pile books, cement blocks, bricks, and so forth on the floor above where you were going to be. You could break open a window and shovel dirt inside. In the basement, you could move chests of drawers and work benches to form a rectangle and, on top of this, pile bags of cement, bags of fertilizer or anything with mass. If there were a vent into the basement, you could shovel dirt from outside in on top of your makeshift shelter.

Figure 10.5

For a makeshift shelter in a home without a basement, you could go in the crawl space beneath the floor and dig a hole, piling the dirt up around. This should be done in a corner where there are no vents. If you were outside and there was no way that you could possibly get to a shelter area, you could drive your car over a ditch and get under it. These solutions are crude, but it is better to lie in a hole for four days and be protected from radiation, than to go out in it and experience a sure death.

Measuring Devices

Important to have in your shelter are two types of measuring devices. The first type is called a dosimeter. There should be at least one for each member of the family. In its most common form, it looks like an oversized fountain pen. This instrument gives the total amount of roentgens that an individual has absorbed. The most common is the 0-200 R dosimeter. The other device is a survey meter, which gives the number of roentgens that are being absorbed per hour. Only one survey meter is needed per shelter. I like to compare these to the speedometer in an automobile. The survey meter tells us how fast we are going and the dosimeter gives the total miles we have come. Both measuring devices are absolutely necessary.

As soon as the nuclear blast occurs, one of the first things that should be done is to give a dosimeter to each individual in the family. Ideally, you would also have one at the office, in addition to an adequate number at home. It is also necessary to have a dosimeter charger. This works on a D battery. Adequate instructions are included with the charger, so there should be no difficulty in using it to recharge the dosimeter.

The survey meter is used to determine hot spots within the shelter. Additional protection can be piled up in that area or, if that is not possible, members of the family can rotate so that each spends an equal amount of time in the hot spots. The survey meter is also necessary to determine when it is safe to go outside. Figure 10.6 shows typical scales on these two devices. Addresses from which these measuring devices can be purchased will be given in Appendix B.

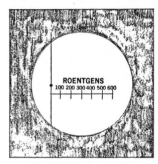

DOSIMETER SCALE

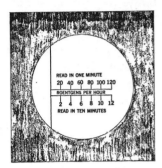

SURVEY METER

Figure 10.6

Leaving the Shelter

Excursions from the shelter *can* be made.   Table 10.2 shows valid reasons for excursions.

If the rate is 60 roentgens per hour (r/hr), a ten-minute excursion will add 10 roentgens to your personal dosimeter.

After making an excursion, it is extremely important not to track any radioactive material into the shelter. Baggies could be placed over your shoes, raincoats could be worn, hats would be essential. Before reentering the shelter, all of these "outside" clothes should be removed. Ideally, the person should strip and wash off thoroughly with water. Any fallout tracked back into the shelter will be damaging to all people inside, as the shelter will not afford protection from radiation within its boundaries.

The canned food in your kitchen will still be good and very usable, even though radiation may have passed through it. This does not harm it at all. If there is any radioactive fallout on the cans, it should be washed off prior to opening them. At some point, it would be wise to wash off the roof of the house to eliminate the roof radiation.   If thought has been given to

Table 10.2

Reasons for Leaving Shelter at Various Radiation Levels	
RADIATION RATE OUTSIDE THE SHELTER (r/hr)	**ACCEPTABLE REASON FOR LEAVING**
MORE THAN 50	Only destruction of the shelter. All other needs must be postponed at least one day.
50 TO 10	Only: a. Destruction of the shelter. b. Removal of dead. c. Severe illness, necessitating immediate treatment with medical help close by.
10 TO 2	a. Obtaining water, if very near. b. Obtaining food, if very near. c. Leaving shelter for nearby shelter with better protection factor.
2 TO 0.5	All rescue, repair, communication and decontamination work. Remain in shelter for sleeping, rest, and meals.
0.5 TO 0	Normal workday can be spent out-of-doors.

this situation beforehand, a small 1-foot square platform could have been erected on top of the house with a lawn sprinkler on it. Between the time of the blast and the fallout, the garden hose could be connected to this, making it easy to wash off the roof.

After the roof is rinsed, the ground at the bottom of the rain gutters will be highly radioactive. As part of the decontamination process, this soil should be scooped out and buried. The soil around your house can be washed off. Check for radioactive hot spots with the survey meter.

Remember that the radioactivity will probably kill most of the animals, both wild and domestic. Protein food will be at a premium after such a nuclear attack. Garden food is still edible, but all radioactive fallout must be washed off. New gardens can be planted. Thus, a can of survival garden seeds is desirable as part of shelter supplies.

Also, it is wise to have stored a bottle of potassium iodine tablets. They keep ingested fallout from being absorbed into the thyroid glad. A typical bottle is a fourteen-day supply. A one hundred-day supply is seven bottles.

PLAN OF ACTION FOR THE HOME

It would be a good idea to develop a plan of action for your family, in case of nuclear war, if you do not already have one. The following are some suggestions for such a plan. During the time between when the blast ocurs and the fallout begins:

1. Extinguish fires.
2. Turn off the main water valve to the house.
3. Put on dosimeters.
4. Place plates outside to detect fallout.
5. Repair shelter damage, finish an incomplete shelter, or create a makeshift shelter.
6. Move water into the shelter. Connect a hose to the hot water drain and put the nozzle inside the shelter.
7. Move canned food from the kitchen to the shelter (leave the food in the freezer).
8. Take the following to the shelter: flashlights, plastic garbage bags and baggies, a battery-powered, all-band radio, bedding, waste elimination system for personal waste and general garbage, books, and recreational materials.

Once you are inside the shelter and the door is closed or, if there is no door, sandbags have been placed across the opening, you should do the following things:

1. Inventory all food and water supplies.
2. Establish a rationing procedure.
3. Delegate important tasks, such as radiation monitoring and food preparation.
4. Set up schedules of eating, sleeping and daily tasks.
5. Establish a schedule for cranking the ventilator fan.
6. Begin constructive activities to occupy the minds of the shelter occupants, to keep them busy.

PLAN OF ACTION FOR THE OFFICE

We have already mentioned that if you are at your office when you see the initial flash, you should crouch behind a desk so that it is between you and the windows on the blast side. Water is going to be important. Therefore, you could go into the washrooms and fill all of the sinks, along with anything else that will contain water (waste basket, pitchers, vases, pencil holders, plastic bags and so forth). If you can get home to take care of your family before the fallout begins, you will probably want to do this. However, for a number of reasons, this may be impossible. It may be that the blast occurred between your office and your home, and the roads are out. It is also unlikely that you will be able to phone your home to find out how they are doing. A quick decision must be made as to whether to try to go home or to remain in the office.

If you decide to remain, you will want to be in one of two places. If it is at an office building, the center of one of the middle floors is quite safe from fallout radiation. The fallout that will land on the top of the building will be stopped by the mass of the floors above you. The radioactive "ground shine" will be below you and you will only be exposed to some radiation from "sky shine." If the building has a subterranean parking lot which goes several floors below the surface of the ground, the bottom floor of that would be fairly safe from radiation. If you go down to the parking lot, carry with you all the water that you can, and anything else that will make life there more comfortable for four days. Having a package of large plastic garbage bags in your desk could be a tremendous help, both for carrying water down to the basement and for use in disposing of human waste.

BOOKS AND INFORMATION

After reading many books on this subject, there is one that I feel is absolutely head and shoulders above everything else that I have read. I think every family should read it. It is *Nuclear War Survival Skills* by Creeson Kearney. Another good book is *Survival Handbook,* by Robert C. Suggs. It covers the entire subject very well. Some of the illustrations and tables in this chapter are taken from it.

There are many booklets available from the Federal Emergency Management Agency. I understand that they are free. Their main publication center is:

Federal Emergency Management Agency (FEMA)
500 C Street SW
Washington, DC 20472   (202) 646-2650

In addition, there are eight regions in the United States designated as the civil defense regions. The following is a list of the region headquarters from which booklets and local information are obtainable:

FEMA Region 1   (617) 223-9540
Room 442 J.W. McCormack Bldg.
Boston, MA 02109

FEMA Region 2   (212) 225-7209
Rm 1336, Federal Plaza
New York, NY 10278

FEMA Region 3   (215) 931-5500
105 S. 7th Street
Philadelphia, PA 19106

FEMA Region 4   (404) 853-4200
1371 Peachtree St. NE—Suite 700
Atlanta, GA 30309

FEMA Region 5   (312) 408-5500
175 W. Jackson Blvd.—4th Fl.
Chicago, IL 60606

FEMA Region 6   (817) 898-5399
Federal Regional Ctr—Rm. 206
Denton, TX 76201

FEMA Region 7   (616) 283-7061
911 Walnut St.—Rm 300
Kansas City, MO 64106

FEMA Region 8   (303) 235-4811
Federal Regional Ctr-Bldg. 105
Denver, CO 80225

FEMA Region 9   (415) 923-7100
Presidio of San Francisco—Bldg. 105
San Francisco, CA 94129

FEMA Region 10   (206) 487-8800
130 228th St. SW
Bothell, WA 98021

From these, you can get a book list and the following free booklets:

H34   *Are you Ready*
          (A Handbook on Disaster Preparation)
H12-1   *Below Ground Home Fallout Shelter*
H12-2   *Above Ground Home Fallout Shelter*
H12-C   *Concrete Block Basement Fallout Shelter*

*H12-4.1 Instructions for Building A Home
Shelter*

For your convenience these addresses will be repeated in Appendix B.

BUILDING OR BUYING
A FALLOUT SHELTER

In many basements, a fallout shelter can be retrofitted. If you are building a home, you can have an extra excavation made so that your basement extends 8- to 12-feet further out than the part of the basement directly under your house. That extended room should have poured concrete walls (if you are in an earthquake or volcanic zone) and a 1-foot poured concrete lid (ceiling). Through the walls, you would want to place vent pipes for both incoming and outgoing air. The incoming air pipe would be the one that would have a blower attached to it to force air from the outside in. On the outside end of that intake vent, you would want to have a fine micron filter to eliminate any radioactive dust from coming into your fallout shelter.

If you are building this from scratch, if at all possible, it would be desirable to have a flush toilet in it and a center floor drain.

If one can afford it, this room could be made into a recreational room—I like to call it a "happy room"—where the family could gather together to play table games, read, and enjoy a quiet evening together. It could have a couple of hide-a-bed couches or even a small kitchen for snacks, and things for normal use other than in times of emergencies. I would personally suggest that you have no television there (you could bring one in during a time of emergency, if you wished), but let this "happy room" be a place where the family could spend a happy family time together at least once a week.

An alternative to building one of your own fallout shelters would be to purchase one. If you do, this is usually of the cylinder-type, frequently made out of old fuel tanks. If you purchase one, they come with many of the desirable features already built into them. All you have to do is to dig a hole and drop it in and cover it up—except for the entrances, of course. Appendix B gives sources for prepackaged disaster (fallout) shelters.

STOCKING AND SUPPLYING
THE STORM SHELTER
OR THE FALLOUT SHELTER

There are many important things that you should include when stocking or supplying your storm shelter or fallout shelter. One ideal would be a top-opening freezer. On a rotating basis, you could keep frozen sandwiches, frozen fried chicken, and other items you could thaw out and immediately eat without cooking. A great deal of cooking in a fallout shelter creates heat and getting rid of this excess heat can be a problem. This food needs to be rotated every six months. By rotating these foods frequently, using the oldest and replacing them with fresh ones, you would ensure that these foods would be in good condition if you were to need them in an emergency situation.

You also need to consider the disposal of human waste, since you may be occupying this shelter for two weeks or more. If you can have a flush toilet, that is wonderful, but if the water is off, that may not work. Every shelter or cellar should have a porta-potty or chemical toilet of some type with an adequate number of plastic garbage bags, so that you could dump out the contents of the porta-potty, tie them up firmly and set them outside the shelter. Additionally, a large garbage can with a very tight-fitting lid would be helpful.

Bedding and sleeping is also a consideration. Sleeping bags and hopefully some pieces of foam on which to put them would be the minimum you would want for sleeping. We just mentioned that if you have a happy room that is a functional room in the house on an everyday basis, you could even have hide-a-beds in there.

You would also want in your shelter the water, lights and first aid kit which were discussed in Chapters 2, 3, and 4.

There are many other important items required in stocking a fallout shelter. We refer you to the excellent video by John and Judy Wadsworth entitled, *"Preparation For Emergencies,"* available from Omega (*B). John is an expert in fallout shelters and he gives details in building a fallout shelter (storm cellar) and shows you the various options you have in stocking it with all the things that you will need in an emergency. This is the very best video we have ever seen on the subject and it could be a real lifesaver to you.

SUMMARY AND CONCLUSION

The final consideration of emergency preparation that we have addressed is providing some form of shelter. Earlier in this century, storm cellars were a common thing in many parts of this country. For many reasons, we have become a nation more and more dependent on others taking care of us and less and less conscious of common sense provisions we can make for ourselves that would help us to fare better through any number of potential disasters that could occur at any time.

Giving thought and attention to providing some type of security shelter is just as wise today as it was in my early days in Texas when the sudden occurrence of a tornado was a very real possibility to be factored into our lives. The profusion of natural and man-made disasters in recent years should underline the fact that careful thought as to how we should prepare should not be something that we allow to be crowed out of our minds and our schedules.

We have discussed a number of approaches that one could take concerning shelter, from a simple, old-fashioned root cellar dug in the back yard to a "happy room" recreational area that is a functional part of the basement in your home. Buying a ready-to-bury shelter is another option. At least under-standing what the real dangers are in case there were ever a nuclear attack on this country helps to prepare you to know what action to take, if you were to find yourself in a situation wherein the best you could do would be to create a makeshift shelter. Knowledge and forethought can also be valuable steps of preparation.

STEP 10: BUY OR BUILD A "HAPPY ROOM" TO SHELTER YOU FROM STORMS AND POSSIBLE FALLOUT.

Before you can know exactly what you need to do to prepare, it is a good idea to find out how prepared you are. The suggestions in the next chapter will help you to determine your current state of preparedness for emergencies.

Chapter 11

FAMILY ACTION PLAN FOR EMERGENCIES

It would be a shame for people to build customized first aid and medical boxes and then not be able to find them during a time of emergency. It would be pitiful if flashlights and emergency lamps had been stored away, but no one could remember where they were and no one had been assigned to be responsible to check the batteries periodically and replace them when necessary. It would be ludicrous if fire extinguishers had been purchased, but they had not been recharged on a regular basis, such that when say, ten-year-old fire extinguishers were grabbed for use in a crisis, they were ineffective.

So, along with making initial preparations, you need to have a family plan on how to keep those preparations current and up-to-date, assigning different individuals to be responsible for the various items of preparation. It is a good idea to have a family meeting every six months to check up on everyone and all of the preparations. It is wise to have a definite family plan of action as to exactly what each person is going to do in a time of emergency.

In this chapter, we will look at developing a Preparation Action Plan (PAP), but first let us consider how prepared we really are.

SHE WENT THROUGH IT!

I would like to share a letter with you from a lady who went though Hurricane Frederick that hit Mobile, Alabama in 1979. Here is what she had to say about her firsthand experience:

Dear James,

This is a postscript to Hurricane Frederick's aftermath in Mobile from one of your subscribers.

Needless to say, this was a brand new experience for most people. Nevertheless, on the whole, the quick response of the Civil Defense, National Guard, law enforcement personnel, elected officials, Board of Health, news media and personnel of the power and phone companies was outstanding. There were some mistakes, goofs such as conflicting information at times, some political bickering and a problem in opening public schools, that kept the schools closed for two weeks.

At no time has the Scripture "joy cometh in the morning" been more meaningful. After the fury of the storm passed, my family walked outside and dug our way through a forest of broken limbs, shrubbery and uprooted trees to a beautiful sunrise but unbelievable devastation. During the night, the "blackness" could only be compared to being deep within a cave as the guide turns off the lights. The roar of the wind was so loud throughout the night that we did not hear the trees cracking or uprooting around us or parts of the neighborhood buildings being blown away. Our world had shrunk overnight to our home and immediate neighborhood and one radio station.

Living on the hill as we do, that first morning we were without power, phone or water. There was no electricity to pump the municipal water up to the higher elevations. There was also hardly any transportation. Our cars, hauling trailer and motorcycle were under the garage that was under a huge oak which would take 21 days to get removed and be able to pull out the repairable car. We did get the motorcycle out the second day—with a dead battery.

Between our home and 250 feet down the street to my Mother's were four impassable areas, even to walking. The devastation to vegetation was shocking. By 7:00 a.m. the air was filled (with) the buzz of chain saws and the task of cleaning up had begun. Later that day our pastor was a welcome sight when he passed by on his way to purchase temporary roofing materials. During the days following our church assumed the function of a clearing house of information to relatives calling from over the country inquiring of their families' welfare.

That first day, we used the bicycle to go to the nearest operating phone some 4 blocks away. A neighbor volunteered a truck, sharing their wheels with us. We ran the truck off of siphoned gas from the cars. Gasoline was probably the second hardest thing to come by. Without electricity the pumps won't operate until generators or hand pumps are installed.

Our personal experience was that we were able to rent a car in 2 days, received running water in 3 days, and were in the lucky 25 percent to have power restored within 4 days. In clean up we found the snakes were more numerous and biting and stinging insects at times almost became a plague. The aloe plant was most useful in relieving pain and itching from yellow jackets speedily.

My husband, Gene, took a week vacation and almost single handedly undertook the job of cleaning the yard. You had to do for yourself as every one was having the same problems.

The Ice Company where I am employed operated by generator brought in by the guard, with rifle bearing guards and police constantly present to prevent any possible riots. (Some of those people were understandably quite rough.) The Civil Defense dispensed free ice throughout the county for over a week until the power was over 50% restored.

Three weeks have now passed and some phones and power are still out and many, many streets are stacked high with highly inflammable vegetative debris. The Corps of Engineers undertook the responsibility of letting out contracts to clear streets and private property for the city, as an aide to existing crews. There are over 3 million cubic feet to be removed. This is one of the biggest helps to those of us that suffered minor damage—minor in comparison to those that lost all their material possessions.

This storm presented an opportunity for us all to learn and grow spiritually and obtain firsthand experience in *physical survival. I became aware of inner weaknesses and strengths within, while trying to cope with a multitude of unfamiliar problems. Reflecting back on the past few weeks, there is great joy as always in seeing one's prayers answered as they were, in seeing God meet any and every personal need. (I hope one of the lessons I learned from Freddie is to pray a more complete prayer. I had neglected to pray for the garage, vehicles or barn and these were what received the damage at our place.) I thank God for the beautiful peace He gives His children and pray for those who say they were so frightened at this time.*

Also, I must tell you that the urging for preparation of emergencies in End-Times News Digest [now titled The Cutting Edge] (*B) were quite helpful. I am sure we were more comfortable for the few preparations we had completed. We had a 55 gal. drum of kerosene with a hand pump (this is my greenhouse heating method), that we were able to share with our neighbors, a supply of lamps, water purifier if needed, and also the survivor saw which I found convenient to use, especially since my husband doesn't allow me to use his chain saw. The Lord provided the chain saw last January. Our cooking was done at Mother's on her propane stove. Frederick won't ever be forgotten by those of us who experienced it.

If you read through this letter, James, what I am really trying to say is a big thank you and to tell you to keep on keeping on preparing us for whatever the future has in store.

Yours in Christ,
Mrs. J.H.C., Mobile, Alabama

As you can tell from this letter, from a person who actually went through a disaster, this lady was very grateful for the preparations that she had made.

One potential item of preparation that we have not mentioned, which is brought to mind by this lady's letter, is a chain saw. If there are trees or telephone poles in your area, during many emergencies these will be toppled and will need to be removed. It would very wise to have a chain saw and to be sure to that you know how to use it. Knowing how to use it would include being able to sharpen the teeth on the chain with a regular chain saw sharpening file or having a self-sharpening chain saw. You would need an amount of gasoline and oil to store in order to drive the chain saw. The amount of gasoline that you can store would vary with city ordinances and your own personal economy.

LEVELS OF PREPARATION

One thing your family should do early on is to decide which level of preparation you feel you should make. Various potential levels of preparation are:

1. Barely survive for three days
2. Survive better for three days
3. Survive with comfort for three days to three months
4. Survive in comfort for a year or more

Of course the ideal, if you can afford it, would be level 4 above. But, it may be that your concern for disasters is low, as well as your finances, and you would be happy if you could make enough preparations to hep you survive for 72 hours and just get by. You might be comfortable with preparing just to level 1.

Another thing to consider in thinking of levels of preparation is how many people are you preparing for? Are you preparing just for those in your immediate family or should you prepare to feed some additional hungry relatives and neighbors? We believe it is wise to lay up some extra supplies for some unexpected mouths that may appear on the scene, looking for you to care for them.

The first 72-hour type preparation should be made immediately and, as far as some of the other areas of preparation discussed in this book, you do not have to do it all the first week. You could gradually accumulate containers in which to store water, For example you could start with a smaller first aid kit and then later move that to the car and acquire or compile a larger one for your home. Whatever you do, it is important to make a plan and to *get started.*

Try to envision yourself in the condition of the lady whose letter you just read. Suppose hurricane (or an earthquake or something else) has just hit your town and laid waste to everything. There is no water, electricity or phones. What would you like to have stored in your own home in that situation? You might sit down and write a list. Whatever is on the list, go purchase it as soon as you can. Then you can stop worrying about disaster preparation.

THE FOOT LOCKER APPROACH

Imagine the following scenario which I like to think of as the Robinson Crusoe approach. If you knew that a ship was going to take you to an undeveloped island where you would have to live for a year, drop you off and come back a year later and pick you up, what would you like take with you? Let's even make the situation a little more exciting and say that this particular island got very cold in the winter and very warm in the summer. Let's say that each member of your family could take two or three footlockers with them. What would you put in those footlockers? What are the essentials that you would like to have with you?

Of course, food for the year would be well in order, since you do not know if that island has anything edible growing on it. A way to purify any fresh water on the island would be worth considering, or perhaps even desalinate the sea water to make drinkable water. Of course, you would want a first aid kit and a medical kit, extra sweaters and coats for the winter, and shorts and swimsuits for the summer.

What if there might be wild animals on the island? You might want to take some means of protecting yourself and your family against wild animals. You would probably want to take either sleeping bags or blankets. The small, lightweight sleeping bags like backpackers use would take up less space.

Would you want to have the ability to grow your own food? Yes, you probably would, so that would mean taking some vegetable seeds with you. To add meat to your stored food, you might want to have a hunting rifle, traps, and fishing tackle.

What if there were natives on the island? Would you like to have some items with which you could barter? You could store some essential things that they would be interested in trading for some of their food, clothes or other items that you might want from them.

If you are going to garden, you would need some gardening tools. For example, you could always take a hoe and a rake, but without handles, planning to find or make wooden handles on the island for these implements. If you are not familiar with gardening, you may want to take some books on gardening and other vital subjects.

You would want to take some sunscreen and maybe a hat to protect you from the harsh sun in summertime.

What about recreation? You might want to take along some books, games, and other recreational equipment. If you include something like a basketball or a football, be sure to include a supply of inflating needles, as well as a pump to keep them inflated.

Your clothes may get torn or worn, so certainly some needles of various sizes and thread would be vital to have.

Just pause and think—what would *you* want in those footlockers, if you were going to go off and live out of those supplies, on your island, having no access to stores for an entire year.

If, per chance, you have a second home that you use for vacations, or have a close relative who lives out in the country, you may actually want to create such emergency footlockers and store them there at the second home or your relatives' home. This is hoping and presupposing that you will be able to get there after a disaster, which may not be that easy. It may be that you want to store these footlockers in your own garage and, if your neighborhood begins to look like a very undesirable place to be, you could always load them all into a trailer and "go west" (or east, north or south—wherever your new home is going to be).

Before we get too far into thinking about preparing or planning for the future, we need to find out how prepared we really are. Thus, we would highly recommend taking the following two-day test.

LET'S TAKE THE TWO-DAY TEST

A disaster could strike your area this Friday at 5:30 p.m., and you could find yourself without water, electricity and gas all weekend. The roads could be impassible, so that you could not go to the drugstore, grocery store or the gas station. If that were the case, you would have to live at least all weekend without being able to make any further preparation.

To test yourself on how prepared you really are, here is what I would challenge you to do (as recommended on Wadsworth's video—*B). This Friday evening at 5:30 p.m. turn off the water and the gas coming into the house, throw the electrical switches in your main electrical box to cut off all electricity to the house, and unplug the telephones.

On Sunday at 5:30 p.m. all of these should be turned back on. Doing this will allow you to find out how you would fare for two days, just 48 hours, without all those utilities and without being able to go to the drugstore, grocery store or gas station. This will show you how prepared you really are and it will clarify dramatically the things that you need to do in order to be more prepared.

If you take this test, you will find that if you do not have some water stored, you will be in trouble. After an earthquake, it might take days to truck water to some areas after an earthquake. For drinking and cooking, allow a minimum of a half gallon (ideally at least a gallon) per person per day. Since there will not be enough water to wash dishes, you will also find that having a supply of paper cups and plates is highly desirable.

I hope you will try this two-day test and will drop me a letter telling me of your experiences. Your letter may be helpful to include in a future edition of this book.

If you are reading this after having done the two-day test, I suspect you found many things that you would have liked to have had and did not have. I admire you for having the "true grit" to go through those two days. I am proud of you. Now that you have discovered the areas where you are lacking, you can more intelligently develop a plan to get from where you are to where you want to be.

A PLAN TO GET PREPARED

The first step is to develop a family plan to get you prepared, because you are going to try this weekend test again two months from now. You need to realistically plan to take that weekend test again, so that everyone in your household will have a sense of urgency and responsibility to accomplish the things that they each need to do.

You can begin to develop your plan by taking a piece of ordinary, ruled notebook paper and drawing a wide column on the left, followed by three columns, each about one-inch wide. Label these four columns: Item, Person Responsible, Date Due, Date Completed. If you wish, you could add a fifth column for Approximate Cost.

Now that you have your "Preparation Action Plan" (PAP) paper ready to go, you need to start with the most important thing that you found was missing. Perhaps it is to "store 55 gallons of water." You would write that under "Item" and then assign a person to be responsible for doing that. Let's just say, "Daddy." Find out when he thinks he can have it done. If he feels he can have that task accomplished in thirty days, you would enter the date of thirty days later under "Date Due." The next item might be "purchase more batteries for flashlight, radio, etc." Your eldest son may be assigned to that, with a due date in two weeks of when he is supposed to have it done. You could go right down the list from the most important tasks down to the least important, assigning a person responsible and a due date.

You need to have one person be the EMERGENCY COORDINATOR (EC). When somebody completes one of his or her tasks, then he or she should tell the Emergency Coordinator, who will then write down the date under the "Date Completed" column of the PAP.   Frequently, the best Emergency Coordinator is a younger child who will pester everyone to death until they get all their assigned tasks done.

So, everybody does what they were assigned to do and two months later, you take the weekend test again. The difference will be like living in a plush mountain retreat versus a pup tent. You will be amazed at what a nice experience that second weekend can be once you have made a few simple preparations.

PREPARATION ACTION PLAN

NO	ITEM	APPROX COST	INDIVIDUAL RESPONSIBLE	DATE DUE	DATE DONE
1.	Store 55 gallons of water		Daddy		
2.	Purchase extra batteries		John		
3.	Increase wet pack food reserves		Mother		

PREPARATION UPDATE
MAINTENANCE PLAN

Once you have made all your wonderful preparations, you need also to be sure that they are maintained. As we have said earlier, you need to be sure that the batteries in the flashlights still work, and fire extinguishers have been recharged within their time limits.

After you make out a list of the things that need to be checked periodically, an individual should be assigned to each of these various tasks, to ensure that they get done. You can keep track of this on a piece of lined paper with columns drawn on it, similar to what we described for your Preparation Action Plan. As you get together once every six months to review this Preparation Update Maintenance Plan (PUMP), each individual should give a report on the things for which he is responsible.

PREPARATION UPDATE MAINTENANCE PLAN

NO	ITEM TO CHECK	DATE LAST CHECKED	INDIVIDUAL RESPONSIBLE	DATE DUE	DATE DONE
1.	Check flashlights	Jan. 1	John	July 1	
2.	Recharge Fire Extinguishers	Jan. 1	Dad	July 1	
3.	Replenish first aid supplies	Jan. 1	Mom	Jul. 1	

For your semiannual meeting to review your PUMP, it is good to pick dates that are easy to remember, such as January 1st and July 4th. Again, you could let one of your children be responsible to start notifying everyone about two weeks ahead of time that the PUMP review is coming up.

HOME EMERGENCY ACTION PLAN

The Home Emergency Action Plan (HEAP) is a plan of action detailing what each person should do during and immediately after an emergency or disaster. Again, take a similar piece of paper, like you have for the other two plans, and write down: Activity and Person Assigned. This could have a number of small columns over to the right of these initial two, showing the dates when each person actually practiced his activity. For example, someone should be assigned to turn off the gas and the water.

A fun thing to do to help familiarize your family members with how to do this expediently is to have a timed race to see who can turn off the water and gas the fastest, for this is something that every member of the family of a reasonable age should know how to do. Someone should be assigned to check for fires. This person should know exactly where the fire extinguishers are and probably should be the person responsible at the PUMP meeting to report on the status of the fire extinguishers (when they were last recharged). Someone needs to be responsible for the flashlights and for getting out the lamps and other lights. You may want to make someone responsible for getting out the stove on which you are going to cook your meals, and so forth.

In addition, a Home Emergency Action Plan (HEAP) should include such things as where to meet if everyone is not at home or gets scattered. Another item that would be good to discuss would be which relative or friend out-of-state everyone could call to let him/her know your whereabouts and your condition following an emergency or disaster. Another item might be who will take over certain responsibilities in case various members of the family are missing or incapacitated.

HOME EMERGENCY ACTION PLAN

NO	ACTIVITY	PERSON ASSIGNED	DATE PRACTICED	DATE PRACTICED
1.	Turn off gas and water	Dad		
2.	Check for fires	John		
3.	Get out emergency lights	Mary		
4.	Get out cook stove	Mom		
5.	Call Aunt Betty out-of-state	Mary		
6.	Back up person for gas/water	John		

Once you have your Home Emergency Action Plan (HEAP), it would be good to practice it, just like children in school have fire drills so that if there actually is a fire, they will all know exactly what to do. It may be that some afternoon the head-of-the-house says, "Emergency Drill! A disaster just hit. Let's put our HEAP into action." Then everyone would do their assigned tasks.   The person in charge of the fire extinguisher would grab the fire extinguisher and pretend to put out an imaginary fire. Someone else would turn off the gas and water into the house. (Yes, I know—you have to relight the hot water heater and the pilots on the stove later, but it is worth it and a good thing to know how to do anyway.) Someone else might grab the first aid box and bring it to the youngest member of the family, who supposedly has broken an arm. He or she could practice making a sling for the arm.

This all may sound a little silly or a bit like the Cub Scouts (no negative reflection on that fine organization), but in recorded cases wherein families have had plans like this, when an emergency did occur, not only were they able to take care of themselves in a wonderful way, but also to help their neighbors. It is worth it, so that family members have something concrete and productive to do in an emergency situation, rather than being paralyzed into inaction due to panic.

SUMMARY AND CONCLUSION

Most people do not know how terribly unprepared for emergencies they are. To find out the true status of your preparedness, we have recommended that you take the 48-hour (weekend) emergency test, by shutting off the gas, electricity and water to your home (and staying home for the weekend, of course) and seeing how everyone fares. After you have done this, you will discover the vital areas in which you need preparation.

We suggest that you draw up a Preparation Action Plan (PAP), in which you assign to various family or household members the items of preparation you need to make and a due date by which they should have each task completed. Once you have your PAP completed, the Emergency Coordinator (EC) will fill in the dates when the tasks are actually completed. Set a goal for yourselves to try the 48-hour test again about two months later, and see the difference a little preparation can make.

After your initial preparation, it is wise to have a semiannual review Preparation Update Maintenance Plan (PUMP) to be sure that all of the items are still in a state of readiness. Batteries in the flashlights should be checked to be certain they are still working. The first aid kit may need to be replenished, if it has been used. Fire extinguishers need to be checked periodically to be sure they are up-to-date and in place.

In addition, your initial Preparation Action Plan (PAP) and your PUMP review meetings, you also need to have a Home Emergency Action Plan (HEAP), so that everyone will know exactly what they are to do when an emergency occurs, without someone having to start yelling out orders in a chaotic situation, adding to the mass confusion. It is good to practice this Family Emergency Plan, probably in connection with your PUMP review.

For your convenience, two full-page copies of each of the three forms described in this chapter are provided at the back of this book.

STEP 11: DEVELOP WRITTEN PLANS FOR PREPARATION, MAINTENANCE AND EMERGENCY ACTION. ALSO CONSIDER BUYING A SMALL ELECTRICAL GENERATOR, A CHAIN SAW AND OTHER SUCH EQUIPMENT.

Even though we discussed electrical generators in Chapter 3, some of the other steps were deemed more important than the purchase of one. That is why it is included again here in Step 11.

A little planning can go along way in helping you meet emergencies victoriously and with ease.

OVERALL SUMMARY

A disaster or an emergency could hit your town or your home at any time. People do not plan to have their homes burn down, but this could happen to any family during any night. Any part of the country could experience a major disaster without warning. Of course, the likelihood of certain types of disasters vary in different parts of the country, but disasters from nature—such as hurricanes, tornadoes, flooding, earthquakes, volcanic eruptions, and fires—can and do strike suddenly. Any preparation that you are going to make for these must be done well ahead of time. Most people realize this, but they really don't know where to start, so they procrastinate and all-too-frequently end up doing nothing. In this book, we have given you a priority sequence of steps to consider taking:

1. Buy provisions for an initial 72 hours.
2. Store adequate water.
3. Provide for light (and heat).
4. Have a good first aid and medical box that is customized to your family.
5. Be prepared to extinguish fires.
6. Decide to what extent you will protect yourself, your family, and/or your property.
7. Store food.
8. Make earthquake preparation.
9. Be prepared to barter for or buy items that you may find that you need and do not have.
10. Provide a storm cellar or fallout shelter, which should be the "Happy Room."
11. Do planning for preparation and emergencies and buy any other desirable equipment.

STEP 1: PURCHASE A 72-HOUR SURVIVAL KIT FOR EACH MEMBER OF YOUR FAMILY. Keep these supplies in your car so they will be with you wherever you are: at home, work, vacation or recreation.

STEP 2: STORE WATER AND BE ABLE TO PURIFY WATER. After almost every disaster, drinkable water is in short supply. To store enough water for a family of four for two weeks requires at least 50 gallons.

STEP 3: PROVIDE FLASHLIGHTS FOR IMME-DIATE USE AND A LONGER-TERM SOURCE OF LIGHT AND HEAT FOR EVENINGS. Having a source of emergency light is particularly important if disasters occur during the night. At least half of the emergencies and disasters do indeed occur at night and with the electricity being disrupted. Thus, you are going to need to have good working flashlights by your bed. If the electricity is going to be off for several days, it seems good to have an alternate source of light such as propane lanterns that you can use to read, cook, and so forth.

If you are in a northern climate area that has cold winters, heat is also a consideration. There are many good propane and kerosene heaters that can be utilized (*B).

STEP 4: PREPARE A FIRST AID BOX AND A MEDICAL BOX, AND LEARN FIRST AID. It is very important to have a good first aid box and a medicine box that is customized to your family. The medical box should contain any prescription drugs upon which the various members of the family rely. The first aid box should contain enough supplies to be able to take care of burns, wounds, and other physical problems that can occur during emergency situations.

STEP 5: BUY ADEQUATE NUMBER OF FIRE EXTINGUISHERS AND ACQUAINT FAMILY MEMBERS WITH THEIR LOCATION AND HOW TO USE THEM. So many disasters are followed by fires from broken gas lines and by fallen electrical lines. Frequently, the community is without water, so extinguishing these fires becomes a real problem. An adequate supply of top-quality fire extinguishers in a home is a real necessity. These must be recharged on a regular schedule. The company that sells you the fire extinguishers will recharge them for you (but *only* if you keep track and take them in to be recharged; you must do your part).

STEP 6: DECIDE HOW MUCH HARM, IF ANY, YOU WOULD BE WILLING TO DO TO AN ATTACKER AND BUY ANY NECESSARY ITEMS OR ACQUIRE ANY NEEDED TRAINING. Since self-defense requires forethought, you may want to take some training and purchase anything that is necessary for you to use for defense. A person needs to determine beforehand how much violence he is willing to exhibit toward someone who is attacking and trying to harm his person or property or those close to him.

It may be that preparation then needs to be made by way of acquiring necessary skills. Preparation can be as simple as buying a can of Body Guard or pepper gas spray to carry in your car, to more involved, such as taking a course in karate or attending a shooting school to learn how to properly handle and use firearms.

STEP 7: ACQUIRE AT LEAST A ONE-YEAR SUPPLY OF LONG-TERM STORAGE FOOD FOR EACH MEMBER OF YOUR FAMILY. I believe that every family needs a good food storage program, but it must be one from which they eat at least one day a week, so that it is continuously refreshed. Some people will be happy with two or three months worth of regular grocery store food (wet pack and frozen). Others will be more comfortable if they have a year's supply of dehydrated and freeze-dried foods. In addition, one can store the basic foods, such as the grains and beans, and have a multi-year supply of foods of these types, if so desired.

STEP 8: EDUCATE YOUR HOUSEHOLD IN EARTH-QUAKE PRECAUTIONS AND SECURE HOT WATER HEATER, TALL FURNITURE AND CUPBOARDS. There are simple things that can be done that could help minimize the damage to your property in the event of an earthquake. You could attach tall items of furniture and the hot water heater to the walls with eye screws and wires. Educating your household members as to what to do if an earthquake occurs is also wise planning.

STEP 9: LAY ASIDE THREE MONTHS OF CASH. IN ADDITION, CONSIDER STORING GOLD COINS OR BARTER ITEMS. You should have two to three months of expenses stored in cash. Some of this can be in currency and some in gold coins. You can lay up items with which to trade (barter). These could prove to be very handy in times of emergency or even in normal times, because people will always need the basic items you have stored. When you consider the factor of inflation, these items will cost progressively more and more, so purchasing them at a low cost will be of benefit to you.

STEP 10: BUY OR BUILD A "HAPPY ROOM" TO SHELTER YOU FROM STORMS AND POSSIBLE FALLOUT. In many disasters, you will still have a structure standing that will provide shelter. However, in hurricanes, tornados and major earthquakes, your home and garage may be flattened or damaged so badly that they are not safe to occupy. Having an underground shelter where one can go in times of disaster makes good sense. If at all possible, it is desirable that this be constructed as an integral part of the house. It can be used as a "family room" or what I like to call a "Happy Room," where the family can meet weekly and enjoy reading, games, crafts, but *not* television.

These are the ten basic preparation items in their priority sequence, so I would encourage you to start with number 1 and work down as far as your inclinations lead you to go.

STEP 11: DEVELOP WRITTEN PLANS FOR PREPARATION, MAINTENANCE AND EMERGENCY ACTION. ALSO, CONSIDER BUYING A SMALL ELECTRICAL GENERATOR, A CHAIN SAW AND OTHER SUCH EQUIPMENT. A family could make many of the preceding preparations, yet in a time of emergency all run around in a panic, not knowing what to do. Then, suddenly everyone may decide to do the same thing, leaving other important things undone. Even if you do not complete all ten steps above, you should do Step 11. I suggest that you first develop a Preparation Action Plan (PAP), whereby you initially take care of any basic preparations your family has not made. Then about every six months, I suggest you have a Preparation Update Maintenance Plan (PUMP) meeting and check to be sure that all of the necessary maintenance is being done on the various preparation items. In addition, I suggested a Home Emergency Action Plan (HEAP), which one could practice at the semiannual maintenance meeting.

Does all of this cause you to think too much about emergencies and disasters? No, it is exactly the opposite. A man with no fire insurance on his home, no fire extinguishers and no garden hose may continually worry about his house burning down. However, if he has fire insurance on his home, has an adequate number of fire extinguishers, garden hoses, and possibly a box of sand to extinguish fires, he does not worry about his house burning down, since he has done what he can to be prepared for the potentiality of a fire.

Similarly, once you make whatever preparations you feel you need to make, concern about disasters and emergencies can be removed from your mind much more so than if you made no preparations whatsoever.

PEACE OF MIND

Everyone wants peace of mind. I believe that following the instructions in this book will help give you some of that peace of mind. I was on a quest for peace for the first twenty-two years of my life. In Appendix A, I share how I found real peace halfway through college.

As we make the preparations that we feel we should make, and we have a right relationship with our God, we can and should live in perfect peace. Our heart should be calm and there should be no fear whatsoever.

Hopefully, this book has caused you to think about various emergencies or disasters that could happen in your community or that would affect your home or family. Once you have made adequate preparations, according to your own goals and comfort level, you will rarely need to think about potential disasters. You can live on hope and real peace of mind, knowing that you have done what you felt you should do to be prepared.

Other Recommended Books in this Series

See the last page of this book, if you wish information on how to obtain a copy of a second book in this "Preparation" series entitled *Self-Reliant Living* (400 pages). It picks up where this books leaves off, covering aspects of having a reliable food supply (such as moving to a farm, having a garden, greenhouse and vineyard, and raising animals), as well as how to make a transition from the city to a small town, a rural community or even how to be more self-reliant in the city. The 10" X 11 1/2" companion book, *Self-Reliant Workbook*, contains about 200 helpful photos and descriptions of how to put many of these ideas into practice.

CHECKLIST

For your convenience, here is a check list for your preparation activities:

_____ 1. We have 72-hour survival kits purchased or made.

_____ 2. Adequate water storage has been made.

_____ 3. Flashlights and longer-term lights and heating stoves are provided.

_____ 4. Customized first aid box and medical box are completed.

_____ 5. Fire extinguishers are in place and current.

_____ 6. Planning and preparation for violence have been made. Any necessary training has been taken.

_____ 7. Adequate food storage has been made and we are regularly using this food.

_____ 8. Preparation for earthquakes has been made; the hot water heater and tall furniture are all secured to the walls.

_____ 9. We have laid up funds or items with which we can barter or buy items that we may need.

_____ 10. An underground shelter has been completed.

_____ 11. Planning has been done and implemented.

       _____ 11.1 A Preparation Action Plan (PAP) has been made.

       _____ 11.2 We have arranged for semiannual review meetings of our Preparation Update Maintenance Plan (PUMP).

       _____ 11.3 We have a Home Emergency Action Plan (HEAP) and all family member know what they are to do in times of emergencies.

Appendix A

HOW I
FOUND PEACE

By Dr. James McKeever

All the world is looking for peace and can't seem to find it. The same thing was true of me as a young person. All of my life, I had been looking for something and had not really known what it was. I vaguely called it *happiness*. When I was in college, I thought, "If I become the best dancer in college, then I will be happy." I did become one of the best dancers in college; in fact, I eventually taught dancing at Arthur Murray's, but after I achieve that, I still felt a bit of an emptiness. Then I thought, "If I get a new convertible, then I will be happy." I got a new convertible and that did not bring me the happiness I was looking for. There was a continual restlessness inside of me. It reminds me of the song that came along later entitled "Is That All There Is?"

As I continued my search for this "something," I started dating a girl who was an excellent dancer and a very beautiful, lovely companion. The major drawback was that she was a Baptist. As a good Methodist boy, I had been warned about the Baptists, that they were narrow-minded, fanatical, and they would try to convert you. She kept pestering me to go to the Baptist Student Union (BSU) meeting with her on the SMU (Southern *Methodist* University) campus. I wanted no part of that, but she kept nagging me about it. Finally, I was either going to have to go to this meeting with her or break up.

So I finally told her, "Okay, I will go to your blankety-blank meeting with you one time, if you will shut your mouth and never mention it again." She readily agreed to this. I went to their meeting and saw what I considered at the time to be the social dregs of the campus. And here I was a big fraternity man, invited to all the sorority dances and so forth. In this group, the girls had stringy hair and wore little or no makeup, and the guys were mostly pansies, not what I considered "real men." I thought, "My gosh, what have I gotten myself into?" However, decided I could take anything for one evening, so I sat there with my arms folded, daring anyone to speak to me or even come near me.

The student who gave the talk that night, Gerry Hassel, was the only one in the group that I could really respect as an individual. He had won photographic contests and so had I. He had won a ping pong championship and so had I. He had lifted weights and so had I. Thus, we had many things in common. Eventually, he was the one who helped me find this missing "thing" that I had been looking for, which I found out was peace with God.

When the meeting started, I was amazed when these students prayed—you could tell they were really talking to God. They were not like the prayers that I had heard most of my life in the Methodist church. They had a quality about them in their relationship to God that I wanted. Being the go-getter type, I was at every meetings they had from then on, both their Wednesday night meetings on campus and the weekend youth revivals that they held in churches in the area surrounding Dallas.

I thought I was a Christian. I had been raised in the Methodist church, had taught Sunday school, had read my Bible, and even believed that Jesus Christ was the Son of God. In fact, I had done everything the Methodist church had told me to do. Gerry asked me if I had been born again. I told him, "Of course." Then he asked me the embarrassing question, "When did it happen?" I said, "I have no idea." He said, "If you don't have any idea when it happened, how do you know that it did?" This caused me to begin to wonder if I really was born again, because by then I knew that, according to Jesus' teachings, one could not enter the kingdom of God unless one had been born again.

Also being a pseudointellectual, I had a million questions for which these kids did not have any answers. I am sure they got tired of seeing me coming toward them. Then one evening at one of their youth revivals, Gerry spoke on these two verses:

16 But I say, walk by the Spirit, and you will not carry out the desire of the flesh.
17 For the flesh sets its desire against the Spirit, and the Spirit against the flesh; for these are in opposition to one another, so that you may not do the things that you please.
—Galatians 5

He depicted this as a tug-of-war between the flesh and the spirit. No one had to ask me—I knew which side of that tug-of-war I was on. I was solidly on the flesh side. Gerry pointed out that as one receives Jesus Christ as his personal Savior and becomes born again, he is then transferred from the flesh side to the Spirit side of the tug-of-war. Then he stated that it is possible to know for sure that you have eternal life, that you are on the Spirit side of the tug-of-war. He read this:

11 And the witness is this, that God has given us eternal life, and this life is in His Son.
12 He who has the Son has the life; he who does not have the Son of God does not have the life.
13 These things I have written to you who believe in the name of the Son of God, in order that you may know that you have eternal life.
—1 John 5

Gerry went on to point out that these things are written to those who believe in the name of the Son of God so that they can know that they have eternal life. It is not a "guess so," "hope so" or "maybe so" situation. We can *know* for certain that we have eternal life and thus have peace with God. He said that in order to get to the point of knowing that we have eternal life, we need to review some basic principles. He then spoke about the following ideas.

First, it is important to know that all things that God created—the stars, trees, animals, atoms and so forth—are doing exactly what they were created to do. That is, everything except man. He pointed out that there was only one verse in the Bible that told us why man was created:

> **7 "...Everyone who is called by My name,**
> **And whom I have created for My glory,**
> **Whom I have formed, even whom I have made."**
> **—Isaiah 43**

This verse says that humans were created to glorify God. Gerry stated that neither himself nor any other human being had glorified God in all their lives, in everything that they had said, done and thought. He said that this gives us the first clue as to what "sin" really is and that we could find out more about it in the following verse:

> **23 ...for all have sinned and fall short of the glory of God,...**
> **—Romans 3**

This verse says that all of us have sinned and we all fall short of the purpose for which we were created—that of glorifying God. There is even a simpler definition of sin. Sin is "living independent of God." Any person who has graduated from high school can choose which college to attend. If he or she makes that decision apart from God, it is "sin." This is the basic problem in the Garden of Eden. Satan tempted Eve to eat the fruit of the tree of "the knowledge of good and evil." He said that if she would do this, she would know good from evil and be wise like God. This means that she could make her own decisions and would not have to rely on God's wisdom and guidance. Gerry said that since we all fit into this category of living independent of God and not glorifying Him in everything that we do, we need to look at the results of this sin.

He asked us what "wages" were, and we could all agree that wages are what you get paid for what you do. Based on that, he then read this verse:

> **23 For the wages of sin is death, but the free gift of God is eternal life in Christ Jesus our Lord.**
> **—Romans 6**

This verse states that the wages of sin is death—eternal spiritual death. Spiritual death is what we get paid for the sin that we do. It also gives us the other side of the coin: that is, that through Jesus Christ, we can freely have eternal life instead of eternal death. Isn't that wonderful?!

Gerry said that this brought us to the place where Jesus Christ fits into this whole picture. He then related a story about a judge in a small town which beautifully illustrated to me the place of Jesus in all of this:

In this small town, the newspapermen were against the judge and wanted to get him out of the office. A case was coming up before the judge concerning a vagrant—a drunken bum—who happened to have been a fraternity brother of the judge when they were at college. The newspapermen thought that this was their chance. If the judge let the vagrant off easy, the headlines would read, "Judge Shows Favoritism to Old Fraternity Brother." If the judge gave the vagrant the maximum penalty, the headlines would read, "Hardhearted Judge Shows No Mercy to Old Fraternity Brother." Either way, they had him. The judge heard the case and gave the vagrant the maximum penalty of thirty days or $300 fine.

The judge then stood up, took off his robe, laid it down on his chair, walked down in front of the bench and put his arm around the shoulders of his old fraternity brother. He told him that as judge, in order to uphold the law, he had to give him the maximum penalty, because he was guilty. But because he cared about him, he wanted to pay the fine for him. So the judge took out his wallet and handed his old fraternity brother $300.

For God to be "just," He has to uphold the law that says "the soul who sins will die." On the other hand, because He loves us, He wants to pay that death penalty for us. I cannot pay the death penalty for you because I have a death penalty of my own that I have to worry about, since I, too, have sinned. If I were sinless, I could die in your place. I guess God could have sent down millions of sinless beings to die for us. But what God chose to do was to send down one person, who was equal in value, in God's eyes, to all of the people who will ever live, and yet who would remain sinless. Jesus Christ died physically and spiritually in order to pay the death penalty for you and me. The blood of Christ washes away all of our sins, and with it the death penalty that resulted from our sin.

The judge's old fraternity brother could have taken the $300 and said, "thank you," or he could have told the judge to keep his money and that he would do it on his own. Similarly, each person can thank God for allowing Christ to die in his place and receive Jesus Christ as his own Savior, or he can tell God to keep His payment and that he will make it on his own. What you do with that question determines where you will spend eternity.

After hearing this story, I realized for the first time why I had to receive Jesus Christ as my personal Savior and how He fit into the overall scheme of things. It was not enough just to believe in "God" in general or even to believe that Jesus Christ was God's only son. I needed to have a personal relationship with Jesus and that would get me to God. In fact, it is the only way to God. Jesus, Himself, pointed this out:

> **6   Jesus said to him, "I am the way, and the truth, and the life; no one comes to the Father, but through Me...."**
> **—John 14**

> **23   Whoever denies the Son does not have the Father; the one who confesses the Son has the Father also.**
> **—1 John 2**

Gerry proceeded to say that we were all at war with God:

> **10   For if while we were enemies, we were reconciled to God through the death of His Son, much more, having been reconciled, we shall be saved by His life.**
> **11   And not only this, but we also exult in God through our Lord Jesus Christ, through whom we have now received the reconciliation.**
> **—Romans 5**

Even though we are at war with God, every human soul longs to be at peace with God. In fact, Saint Augustine said that there was a God-sized vacuum in every man's heart that could only be filled by Jesus Christ. I knew then that I wanted to be at peace with God and that the answer was in coming to Him through Jesus Christ and receiving Him as my personal individual Savior:

> 16   "For God so loved the world, that He gave His only begotten Son, that whoever believes in Him should not perish, but have eternal life...."
>
> —John 3

Here we see that if we believe in Christ, we won't perish; we will have everlasting life instead. The way we do this is very simple: we believe in our heart and we confess it with our mouth.

> 9   ...that if you confess with your mouth Jesus *as* Lord, and believe in your heart that God raised Him from the dead, you shall be saved;...
>
> —Romans 10

Gerry went on to say that you cannot come to Christ just as your Savior—you must also accept Him as your Master and be willing to follow Him. That night I knew that I wanted to have peace with God and I wanted to have Christ as my Savior, so I prayed a simple little prayer and asked Christ to come into my heart, to forgive my sins, to take charge of my life and I said I would follow Him.

All of a sudden, a perfect peace like I had never known flooded my entire being. That peace has been with me ever since. I have been up to the heights and have crashed down and been up to the heights again; yet I have had peace through it all. It is a peace that we can have, no matter what turbulent events we are in or what is facing us. It is the kind of peace that Jesus had the night before He was going to be tortured to death. He told this to the disciples in the upper room during the last supper:

> 27   "Peace I leave with you; My peace I give to you; not as the world gives, do I give to you. Let not your heart be troubled, nor let it be fearful...."
>
> —John 14

That peace from Jesus Christ, the Prince of Peace, is something that abides with you. It is a precious gift from Him.

During the 1929 stock market crash and the 1930's, many people committed suicide because their lives were built around material things and, when these were gone, life had no meaning. I would encourage you to seek that peace with God in whatever way you want to seek it. I have found it through a personal faith in Jesus Christ and following Him.

If you decide to pray and receive Christ as your Savior—to and invite Him into your heart and life to forgive your sins and to help you turn from your sins—and you make the choice to follow him, I would love to hear from you. There is a little book I would like to give you that will help you.

If you are still sincerely seeking this peace with God, there is a minibook that I have authored, entitled *Where Will You Be In 300 Years?*, that I will be happy to send to you as my gift, with no strings attached. So I would love to hear from you too. My address is at the end of this book.

May God bless you and give you the peace of Jesus.

Appendix B

INFORMATION AND EQUIPMENT SOURCES

In this appendix, we will give the names and addresses of the various sources for food, equipment, videos, books and so forth. The reason for bringing them all together in this appendix is both for your convenience and to make it easier to update the book in subsequent printings.

First we will list the companies in alphabetical order, giving their addresses, phone numbers and brief descriptions. The next section will list the various products and services grouped by chapters, giving only the names of the companies.

ADDRESSES

We would suggest that you first contact the following organizations to get their catalogs:

> Excalibur Dehydrators
> ICA (International Collectors Association)
> Millennium Outfitters
> Nitro-Pak Preparedness Center
> Oregon Institute of Science and Medicine
> Safe-Trek Outfitters
> Safety Zone
> The Survival Center
> The Urban Homemaker

Sometimes there is a small fee for the catalog, which is usually refunded with the first purchase.

The various organizations are listed in alphabetical order with addresses in this first section. In the following section of this appendix, which is oriented by chapter and product, only the name of the organization (vendor) is listed. So here are the long-awaited addresses:

The Cutting Edge	(541)826-9877
The Cutting Edge Ministries	FAX (541)826-1023
P.O. Box 1788	Email: CEnewsltr@aol.com
Medford, OR 97501	Orders only: (800)343-1111
	Website: htp://www.HDE.org

The Cutting Edge, mentioned on page 150 of Chapter 11, is a 24-page monthly Christian newsmagazine that I (Jeani) edit (formerly edited by James and myself as *End-Times News Digest* since 1980). It is available for a contribution of $30 for a year. It offers hope, direction and encouragement, articles by noted leaders that equip people for spiritual maturity, along with relevant news, updates on world conditions, and a prophetic outlook. It can be an important voice or watchman for you on the cutting edge, during these challenging days in which we live. You can contact this address for a sample issue or send in a contribution ($30 a year) to receive the newsletter regularly.

Essential Oils Healthline	(602)430-7700
P.O. Box 17137	
Fountain Hills, AZ 85269	

An addition since the first edition of this book that I (Jeani) would recommend for your Emergency Medical Box would be some basic ***essential oils***. Essential oils are one of the oldest and most respected medicines known to mankind. Historical records indicate that they were an important therapy in daily life in Egypt, India, and China.

You can think of essential oils as being the lifeblood or the immune system of plants, flowers, trees and shrubs. When we cut our finger, blood cleanses the cut, protects the wound, fights harmful microorganisms, and provides oxygen and nourishment for cell regeneration. The same event occurs in the plant kingdom. The clear liquid that seeps from a cut plant is called the essential oil. These oils are highly antibacterial, antiviral, antifungal, antimicrobial, and yeast inhibiting.

Also of significance, bacteria and viruses do not become immune to essential oils like they do to antibiotics, nor do they harm healthy tissue, as antibiotics can when overused. Because of their highly oxygenating molecular structure, essential oils help to nourish, strengthen, support and restore the body at the cellular level.

During the time of Christ, essential oils were so precious that they were bartered like gold. If you recall, the three gifts that the magi brought to the Christ child were *frankincense*, gold and *myrrh* (two of which were essential oils!–Matthew 2:11). The Bible contains well over 100 references to essential oils, frankincense alone appearing 17 times!

Essential oils are a valuable God-given tool to aid in healing and bringing the body back into balance. Since they require no refrigeration and very little shelf space, they are also good to have on hand for barter or trade purposes. To try some essential oils, I would recommend contacting Essential Oils Healthline for top-quality, high-grade oils, which does make a difference in effectiveness, compared to some brands sold at health food stores.

A company called Young Living (accessed through Essential Oils Healthline) has put together various kits and combinations to introduce people to high-quality essential oils. For example, they offer an "Essential 7 First Aid Kit," which I would recommend personally. I have had good benefit with some basic blends of oils in it, especially one called "Pane Away" (for reducing inflammation and pain from arthritis, sprains, bruises, sore muscles, etc). Another blend called "Peace and Calming" (good for hyperactive children or adults, anxiety, depression, etc.), I have also found to be helpful as a sleep aid.

For a more complete selection of quality oils and oil blends, Essential Oils Healthline offers: 1) The Small Family Kit, 2) The Growing Family Kit, 3) The Ultimate Family Kit, in different price ranges. Again, my personal experience has been very good with the oils I have tried. If you believe—as I do—in the wisdom of taking responsibility for your own health and learning to use preventative health tools available to us, you may wish to become more familiar with essential oils and possibly add some to you own Emergency Medical Box. If you mention that you heard about Essential Oils Healthline through this book, they will be happy to do what they can to introduce you further to these amazing substances.

Excalibur Dehydrators—Dept. SR1   (800)875-4254
6083 Power Inn Road
Sacramento, CA 95824

Excalibur Dehydrators are available in 4-tray, 5-tray or 9-tray sizes, with or without an automatic timer (except for the 4-tray size). These are of top quality and are the best in efficiency of drying time, since the air comes from the back. Because of this horizontal air flow (as opposed to the heat/air source being at the bottom with many brands), there is no need to rotate the trays partway through for even drying. Also, because they are constructed in an oven-like fashion, you can take out every other tray in order to dry large items, like dough art or drying flowers, if you wish to use it for craft projects of that type. This is my (Jeani's) favorite dehydrator (although the Magic Aire dehydrator has a different advantage—see Kitchen Specialties/Bosche Kitchen Center).

Federal Emergency Management Agency (FEMA)
500 C Street SW   (202) 646-2650
Washington, DC 20472

FEMA Region 1   (617) 223-9540
Room 442 J.W. McCormack Bldg.
Boston, MA 02109

FEMA Region 2   (212) 225-7209
Rm 1336, Federal Plaza
New York, NY 10278

FEMA Region 3   (215) 931-5500
105 S. 7th Street
Philadelphia, PA 19106

FEMA Region 4   (770) 220-5224
1371 Peachtree St. NE—Suite 700
Atlanta, GA 30309

FEMA Region 5   (312) 408-5500
175 W. Jackson Blvd.—4th Fl.
Chicago, IL 60606

FEMA Region 6   (940) 898-5297
Federal Regional Ctr—Rm. 206
Denton, TX 76201

FEMA Region 7   (816) 283-7061
911 Walnut St.—Rm 300
Kansas City, MO 64106

FEMA Region 8   (303) 235-4812
Federal Regional Ctr—Bldg. 105
Denver, CO 80225

FEMA Region 9   (415) 923-7100
Presidio of San Francisco—Bldg. 105
San Francisco, CA 94129

FEMA Region 10   (425) 487-4605
130 228th St. SW
Bothell, WA 98021

Available from FEMA are these free booklets:

L154   *Emergency Preparedness Checklist*
            (Item #8-0872)

L191	*Emergency Preparedness Publications* *(Item #8-0822)*
L191	*Your Family Disaster Plan* *(Item #8-0954)*
L189	*Your Family Disaster Supplies Kit* *(Item #8-0941)*
L215	*Emergency Food and Water Supplies*
H34	*Are you Ready?* *(A Handbook on Disaster Preparation)*
H12-1	*Below Ground Home Fallout Shelter*
H12-2	*Above Ground Home Fallout Shelter*
H12-C	*Concrete Block Basement Fallout Shelter*
H12-4.1	*Instructions for Building A Home* *Shelter*

Gunsite Training Center   (602)636-4565
Richard Jee, CEO
Box 700
Paulden, AZ 86334

Gunsite Training Center, founded by Jeff Cooper, offers on-site gun training that is head and shoulders above any other course. There are beginning and advanced courses in handguns and rifles. Training also includes hands-on exercises where you practice shooting the bad guys and not shooting the good guys. If you plan to use firearms for defense, this training is a must.

International Collectors (ICA)   (800)525-9556
Don McAlvany   (303)259-4100
166 Turner
Durango, CO 81301

ICA is an excellent company that has been shipping gold and silver coins nationwide since 1971. They are specialists in both bullion and numismatic coins. There is an advantage to having these shipped to you from Durango, Colorado. In that no local coin company knows that you have them.

ICA is reputable and reliable and we do not hesitate to recommend them. They have a minimum order size of $1,000. Its President, Don McAlvany, is an outstanding Christian man and patriot, whom we have known for over twenty years. Let ICA know that you heard of them through an Omega book.

Kitchen Specialties	(801)263-8900
3767 S. 150 E.	FAX (801)263-8902
Salt Lake City, UT 84115	

Kitchen Specialties is a wholesale company that manufactures and distributes many excellent mills for grinding wheat and other grains. They also produce the Magic Aire food dehydrator.

The Magic Aire dehydrator has an advantage in that, although the air comes up from the bottom, it has stackable trays, and you can remove unused trays, thus shrinking the size of the dehydrator on your counter, if you are not drying a full load. The basic unit comes with eight trays. A dehydrating cookbook, mesh inserts, and fruit leather trays can also be ordered. If additional trays are desired, they can be purchased individually. I (Jeani McKeever) have used this dehydrator very effectively for years with up to ten trays on it.

However, Kitchen Specialties does not sell to individuals, but only through a limited number of retail outlets nationwide. Therefore, let us provide for you the name of a distributor you can contact. As well as excellent equipment, I have also found their prices are lower than most, which could provide a significant savings. If you let them know you read about it in this book, they will also cover your freight on any appliance you order.

Bosche Kitchen Center	(800)950-9109
Bob Hair, President	(801)562-1212
8926 S. 700 East	bkc400@aol.com
Sandy, UT 84070	

As well as the Magic Aire Food Dehydrator, Bosche Kitchen Center carries another dehydrator called the Aire Preserve II. It also has stackable trays, but it is round versus rectangular.

In addition, they carry a high-quality mill called the Whisper Mill with a stainless steel, patented "Microburst" milling chamber. It has all of the advantages of the old stone mills but none of their problems and is an advanced way to mill grain today. It is advertised that it will not overheat and it gives a lifetime of trouble-free service.

Melaleuca Oil Products

Radiance Enterprises   (702)329-2543
9945 Biscayne Lane
Las Vegas, NV 89117

or

Melaleuca, Inc.   (800)282-3000
3910 South Yellowstone Hwy (208)522-0700
Idaho Falls, ID 83402-6003

Since Melaleuca Oil, and other products produced by Melaleuca Inc. which contain the oil, are sold through distributors, we are providing you with one address to contact to enroll in order to be able to make your own purchases at a discounted price directly from the company. As a back up, the company name and phone number are also given. (See page 54 for the benefits of Melaleuca oil and why we would recommend it as a wise addition to your first-aid box.)

Millennium Outfitters L.L.C.   (541)862-2486
P.O. Box 51   (541)865-3370
Butte Falls, OR 97522

Millennium Outfitters is a new addition since the first printing of this book. It was formed in response to the need for public preparedness in the face of potential Y2K-based disruptions in the deliveries of basic goods and services. Founder, Rocky Cowie, is an expert on food storage, emergency medicine (a practicing EMT for fifteen years), rural homesteading and self-sufficiency with a wealth of personal experience in all of these areas. He feels that our best defense against a critical threat to our life support systems (a breakdown of energy, communication and transportation systems) is to become self-sufficient with respect to vital commodities such as water, food, heat and light. However, that type of personal preparation is not enough. Unless one's neighbors and community are prepared, security is seriously compromised.

Millennium Outfitters was formed out of this awareness. They offer a product line of high quality system components for self-sufficient living, addressing areas such as electric generators, fuel storage systems, water purification and water storage systems, food dehydration and food storage systems, grain grinders and other food processors, human-powered appliances, non-electric lighting systems, sprouting accessories, communication devices, medical kits, portable shelters and other critical items.

Nitro-Pak Preparedness Center	(800)866-4876
151 N. Main	FAX (800)654-3860
Heber, UT 84032	www.nitro-pak.com

Nitro-Pak Preparedness Center is a customer-service-oriented company. It has become the nation's largest one-stop source for acquiring most of the preparedness items you will need for the troubling times ahead. They carry a wide line of helpful equipment for surviving short-term or long-term emergencies or crises.

You will find in their catalog such products as:

1. Water storage containers, filters and tablets
2. Complete 72-hour survival kits
3. A selection of preparedness books and videos
4. Wheat mills and mixers
5. Emergency light and heating products
6. Military MRE's (meals-ready-to-eat)

7. Emergency food reserve units from two weeks to one full year and a selection of tasty dehydrated and freeze-dried foods. (They offer exclusively the Nitro-Pak brand of dehydrated foods, as well as Mountain House No-Cook Freeze-Dried Foods.)
8. A wide range of first-aid supplies
9. Self-protection chemical sprays

Their catalog is $3, but with it they give you a $5 certificate that you can use on your first purchase. If you let them know that you heard about them from Omega, they will extend to you a *5 percent discount* on your order. Most orders are shipped within 5-7 days. (This is good to know, as delivery time has become a significant consideration with storage foods.)

Nutri-Flow   (800)290-8435
14200 N.W. Melody Lane   (503)645-9741
Portland, OR 97229-4360

We cannot speak from experience about Nutri-Flow's dehydrator, but it is another alternative of a large-capacity dehydrator with air flow from the back. You can call or write for their free brochure.

Omega Publications and Videos   (541)826-4512
P.O. Box 4130   Email: omegapublications@juno.com
Medford, OR 97501   Orders only (800)345-0175

Omega is a book publisher. They also offer the following video titles that were recommended in various chapters:

Preparation for Emergencies by John and Judy Wadsworth
Dehydrating Made Easy by Jeani McKeever-Harroun
Canning is Fun by Jeani McKeever-Harroun
Vital Food Storage by Dr. Barbara Fair

Omega Publications and Videos has an entire video series available on practical information and skills entitled, *The Growin' Tapes.* Subjects in this ever-expanding series include gardening, canning, dehydrating, food storage, nutrition, healthy living, emergency medicine and other aspects of practical preparation. You can request their complete listing of videos and books when you write or call.

Oregon Institute of Science and Medicine
Arthur Robinson, PhD   (541)592-4142
2251 Dick George Road
Cave Junction, OR 97523

Dr. Robinson is an expert in fallout shelters and has plans for shelter designs and consulting available. He has authored the book about civil defense entitled *Fighting Chance* and published a very helpful resource book entitled *Nuclear War Survival Skills* by Kresson Kearney. You can call or write for a free catalog of other preparedness materials, videos and other publications.

Safe-Trek Essentials   Orders (800)671-3032
90 Safe Trek Place   (406)587-5571
Bozeman, MT 89718   FAX (800)671-9958

Safe-Trek Outfitters   (800)424-7870
Stephen Quayle   (406)587-5571
90 Safe Trek Place   FAX (406)586-4842
Bozeman, MT 59718   Email: safetrek@avicom.net

Safe-Trek is probably the most complete supply center. Safe-Trek Outfitters has an extensive line of water purifiers, MRE's, long-term storage foods, chemical sprays and much more. They have the broadest variety of 72-hour survival kits we have seen. There is one with the basic minimum for one person. Then they have progressively expanded ones, which include medical supplies and many things such as mouthwash, playing cards, a whistle and flares. They also have various expanded packages that will support two, five or ten people for three days. They have a great selection of first aid kits, many of them specifically designed for various conditions. They also have a vast line of medical supplies. In addition, they carry a large selection of books on survival.

As you can see, we could go on and on about the many things that Safe-Trek offers, but it is all contained in their beautiful 103-page (11" x 15") catalog, which has a full-color cover. They charge $8 for it, but it well worth the price for your education in knowing what is available. They will credit the $8 back against your first purchase. If you tell them you are calling or writing because you read about them in an Omega book, they will give you a *10 percent discount* off anything in their catalog.

Safe-Trek Essentials is a sister company that can also handle your precious metal needs (gold, silver, platinum coins). Call for more information.

Safety Zone   (800)999-3030
2515 East 43rd Street   FAX (615)867-5318
P.O. Box 182247
Chattanooga, TN 37422-7247

Safety Zone has a very extensive line of home safety and home security products. Their product line also includes items for car safety and personal protection, as well as a comprehensive array of items for child safety. They handle excellent equipment and have a 55-page, full-color catalog, which is free.

The Survival Center, Dept. 190   (800)321-2900
P.O. Box 234   Email: sales@survivalcenter.com
McKenna, WA 98558   www.survivalcenter.com

The Survival Center is one of the oldest continually operating business that sells storage foods in the U.S. As well as selling grains and beans in nitrogen-packed, 6-gallon buckets, mills, food dehydrators, herbs, water purification equipment, and so forth, they also have knowledge and experience in installing complete underground shelters. They have a large selection of books (including many metaphysical books). Their catalog is available for $2.

The Urban Homemaker   (303)750-7230
P.O. Box 440867   Orders (800)552-7323
Aurora, CO 80044

The Urban Homemaker is a back-to-basics company which handles bread baking equipment and supplies and other preparedness products and resources for preserving foods, dehydrating, water purification, herbal remedies and more. They publish a new catalog of over 50 pages about three times a year.

PRODUCTS BY CHAPTER

In this section we will be listing the companies who sell the various products that have been mentioned throughout the book. This section is oriented by chapter, for your convenience.

Some of the videos mentioned in this section can be rented from Blockbuster or your local video store. However, these are instructional tapes that you will need to view many times, so it may be cheaper to go ahead and purchase them.

Some of the companies listed sell more than what we have indicated here. This is why we encourage you to get their catalogs. Also, we are presenting here the one or two companies that we would use to buy certain items. For example, many of the companies handle first aid kits, but we have just shown the one with the best and biggest selection.

CHAPTER 1—72-HOUR SURVIVAL KITS

72-Hour Survival Kits

Emergency Essentials
Safe-Trek Outfitters
Nitro-Pak Preparedness Center

Book

The Future Revealed by Dr. James McKeever
Available from Omega Publications

CHAPTER 2—WATER

Water Storage Containers

The Survival Center
Nitro-Pak Preparedness Center

Water Purifiers and Pouches of Water (Filled)

Safe-Trek Outfitters
Millennium Outfitters
Nitro-Pak Preparedness Center

Desalinators (Water Purifiers)

Safe-Trek Outfitters

Water Disinfectant Crystals (Polar-pure)
(The one the McKeevers have used when traveling)

Nitro-Pak Preparedness Center

CHAPTER 3—LIGHT AND HEAT

Gas and Water Shut Off Multitool

Nitro-Pak Preparedness Center

Solar-Powered Battery Rechargers

Nitro-Pak Preparedness Center

Kerosene (Aladdin) Lamps and Heaters

Nitro-Pak Preparedness Center

Snaplights (Chemical lights)

Nitro-Pak Preparedness Center

Flashlights

Local sources

CHAPTER 4—FIRST AID

Videos

CPR: The Way to Save Lives J.D. Heade Company	(800)622-5689
Dr. Heimlich's Home First Aid MCA Home Video	(818)777-4300
Emergency Action First Aid ActiVideo	(312)404-0030
First Aid and Emergency Medicine Omega Publications and Videos	(800)345-0175
How to Save Your Child's Life Xenon Video	(310)451-5510

First Aid and Medical Kits

Essential Oils Healthline
Millennium Outfitters
Safe-Trek Outfitters

Herbal Medicine Kits

Safe-Trek Outfitters

CHAPTER 5—FIRE FIGHTING AND DETECTION

Fire Extinguishers

See Yellow Pages

Videos

Fire Safety For the Family Academy Entertainment Inc.	(802)985-2060

CHAPTER 6—SELF-DEFENSE

Chemical Sprays (OC, pepper spray, is preferred)

Safe-Trek Outfitters
Nitro-Pak Preparedness Center

Training for Use of Weapons

Gunsite Training Center

Books

Safe-Trek Outfitters

Personal Safety Products

Safe-Trek Outfitters
Safety Zone

Home Security and Child Safety

Safety Zone

Safes (Disguised as Books and Cans)

Safety Zone
Nitro-Pak Preparedness Center

Safes (Regular with combination)

Safety Zone

Videos

Escape! Prevent Assaults
Simitar Entertainment, Inc.   (612)559-6660

Lisa Sliwa's Common Sense Defense
Vestron Video

CHAPTER 7—FOOD SOURCES

For further discussion of fasting, mentioned briefly in Chapter 7, there is an entire chapter written on the subject in the book entitled *Become Like Jesus,* available (for $10 plus $3 S&H) from:

Omega Publications and Videos

Complete Freeze-dried Food Storage Systems

International Collectors Associates (ICA)
Nitro-Pak Preparedness Center

No Cook Foods (Freeze-dried Prepared Meals)

International Collectors Associates (ICA)
Nitro-Pak Preparedness Center

Dehydrated Food Sources

Safe-Trek Outfitters
Nitro-Pak Preparedness Center

Dehydrators

Three possible choices of good-quality dehydrators that we could recommend from personal experience would be the following:

1. Excalibur Dehydrator–9 tray
2. Excalibur Dehydrator–5 tray
   Both are available through Excalibur.
3. Magic Aire II Dehydrator
   Available through Kitchen Specialties/
   Bosche Kitchen Center.

In addition, Bosche Kitchen Center offers the Aire Preserve II, which we understand is also a good choice.

Grains and Beans for Bulk Storage, Containers

Millennium Outfitters
   (Storage buckets and instruction)
Nitro-Pak Preparedness Center
The Survival Center

Military MRE's (Meals Ready to Eat)
Safe-Trek Outfitters
Nitro-Pak Preparedness Center

Mills

Kitchen Specialties/Bosche Kitchen Center
Millennium Outfitters
The Urban Homemaker

Stoves (portable)

Safe-Trek

Videos—On Food Preservation and Storage

1. *Canning is Fun!* by Jeani McKeever-Harroun
2. *Dehydrating Made Easy* by Jeani McKeever-Harroun
3. *Vital Food Storage*
   by Master Gardener, Dr. Barbara Fair
4. *Food Storage 101* by Rocky Cowie and others
5. *The Y2K Family Preparedness Video Series* (and *Y2K National Yellow Pages* of sources)

Available through Omega Publications and Videos

Books on Dehydrating

1. *Dehydration Made Simple* (Kitchen Specialties/ Bosche Kitchen Center)
2. *Preserve It, Naturally!* (Excalibur Dehydrators)

Low-Cost Food Storage Article

Reprints of the entire article by Jeani McKeever entitled, *"Low-Cost Food Storage and How to Use It"* are available from Omega ($2 each or 3 for $5).

Cookbook

Cooking with Home Storage
(available from Nitro-Pak Preparedness Center)

CHAPTER 8—EARTHQUAKES

Video

Nitro-Pak Preparedness Center

Books

Survival Center

CHAPTER 9—BARTER

Essential Oils

Essential Oils Healthline

Gold Coins, Silver Coins

International Collectors Associates (ICA)
Safe-Trek Essentials

Food

International Collectors Associates (ICA)
Nitro-Pak Preparedness Center
Safe Trek Essentials

Nails, Soap, Shampoo, Toilet Tissue, Bullets

Local Sources

Supplements

Safe-Trek Essentials

CHAPTER 10—A DISASTER (FALLOUT) SHELTER

Video

Preparation for Emergencies
by John and Judy Wadsworth
Omega Publications and Videos

Gas Masks, Nuclear, Biological and Chemical Suits

Safe-Trek Outfitters

Toilets

Sears

Clear Plastic Sheeting (Heavy-mil roll)

Local home improvement stores

Consulting

Oregon Institute of Science and Medicine
Survival Center

Book

Nuclear War Survival Skills
by Kesson Kearney
Oregon Institute of Science and Medicine

ADDITIONAL REFERENCES

Y2K Update Information

Millennium Outfitters

CONCLUSION

Companies do move locations and change phone numbers periodically. If there was a pink slip in the front of this book giving new addresses, please take a pen and make those changes here in Appendix B.

Complete books on most of the individual subjects covered in this volume can be obtained from Safe-Trek Outfitters.

In addition, we would highly recommend to you the second book in this preparation series, *Self-Reliant Living* and its companion workbook, *The Self-Reliant Workbook.* Concerning personal preparedness—whether it be in the city, in a small town or in the country—those more detailed resources pick up where this book leaves off.

Appendix C

MEET THE AUTHORS
Dr. James and Jeani McKeever

Dr. James McKeever is a retired international consulting economist, lecturer, author, world traveler, and Bible teacher. His financial consultations were utilized by scores of individuals from all over the world who sought his advice on investment strategy and international affairs.

Dr. McKeever and his wife, Jeani live on a 70-acre ranch in Oregon, which is basically self-reliant. They have their own water supply, long-term electricity generating capacity and the ability to live with or without electricity. Not only do they grow a garden each year, but they raise sheep for meat and wool, goats for milk and chickens for meat and eggs. They have to dispose of their own trash and concern themselves with other such services that are provided for you in towns and cities. Much of the content of this book is derived from their own experiences or, if it is not something they have tried personally, things they have thoroughly investigated. They come to this subject with a vast background of experience and have been writing about it for over twenty years.

Dr. McKeever was the editor and major contributing writer of the *Money Strategy Letter*, an economic and investment letter with a worldwide circulation and recognition. It was rated number one for three out of four years by an independent newsletter-rating service, and its model portfolio showed an average profit of over 63 percent per year over a period of eleven years.

Dr. McKeever has been a featured speaker at monetary and investment conferences in London, Zurich, Bermuda, Amsterdam, South Africa, Australia, Singapore and Hong Kong, as well as all over the North American continent and Latin America.

As an economist and futurist, Dr. McKeever has shared the platform with such men as Ronald Reagan, Gerald Ford, Henry Kissinger, Oliver North, Alan Greenspan, William Buckley, heads of foreign governments, and many other outstanding thinkers.

For five years after completing his academic work, Dr. McKeever was with a consulting firm which specialized in financial investments in petroleum. Those who were following his counsel back in 1954 invested heavily in oil.

For more than ten years he was with IBM, where he held several key management positions. During those years, when IBM was just moving into transistorized computers, he helped that company become what it is today. With IBM, he consulted with top executives of many major corporations in America, helping them solve financial, control and information problems. He has received many awards from IBM, including the "Key Man Award" and the "Outstanding Contribution Award." His books and articles on computers were translated into many languages.

In addition to this outstanding business background, Dr. McKeever is an ordained minister. He was pastor of Catalina Bible Church for three and a half years (while still with IBM) and is a frequent speaker at Christian conferences. He has the gift of teaching, an in-depth knowledge of the Bible, and has authored twenty-three Christian books, nine of which have won the prestigious "Angel Award."

Dr. McKeever is president of Omega Ministries, which is a nonprofit organization. He is the editor of their widely-read newsletter, *End-Times News Digest,* which relates the significance of current events to biblical prophecy and to the body of Christ today. The worldwide outreach of Omega Ministries is supported by the gifts of those who are interested.

Mrs. Jeani McKeever is an outstanding individual in her own right, as well as the editor of her husband's many books and articles. She is the author of the award-winning book, *Fit as a Fiddle* and is the editor of a popular, monthly health and nutrition column, *"Temple Tips."* She has recorded two music albums of Christian songs and is in demand as a soloist at Christian events. She has made four video tapes on health, nutrition, canning, dehydrating and other vital subjects, and has practical experience in all of these areas and many more. She speaks to Christian ladies' groups on a variety of spiritual and physical subjects.

Together, the McKeevers bring over forty years of experience in the area of preparation and they are glad to share their knowledge and experience with you to help you prepare.

Appendix D
TIPS FROM FEMA
(Federal Emergency Management Agency)

Nutrition Tips

In a crisis, it will be vital that you maintain your strength. So remember:

- Eat at least one well-balanced meal everyday.
- Drink enough liquid to enable your body to function properly (two quarts a day).
- Take in enough calories to enable you to do any necessary work.
- Include vitamin, mineral and protein supplements in your stockpile to assure adequate nutrition.

If the Electricity Goes Off...

First, use perishable food and foods from the refrigerator.

Then use foods from the freezer. To minimize the number of times you open the freezer door, post a list of freezer contents on it. In a well-filled, well-insulated freezer, foods will usually still have ice crystals in their centers (meaning the foods are safe to eat) for at least three days.

Finally, begin to use non-perishable foods and staples.

Family Disaster Supply Kit

It's 2:00 a.m. and a flash flood forces you to evacuate your home—fast. There's no time to gather food from the kitchen, fill bottles with water, grab a first-aid kit from the closet and snatch a flashlight and a portable radio from the bedroom. You need to have these items packed and ready in one place before disaster hits.

Pack at least a three-day supply of food and water, and store it in a handy place. Choose foods that are easy to carry, nutritious and ready-to-eat. In addition, pack these emergency items:

- Medical supplies and first aid manual
- Hygiene supplies
- Portable radio, flashlights and extra batteries
- Shovel and other useful tools
- Money and matches in a waterproof container
- Fire extinguisher
- Blanket and extra clothing
- Infant and small children's needs (if appropriate)

Storage Tips

- Keep food in the driest and coldest spot in the house—a dark area if possible.
- Keep food covered at all times.
- Open food boxes or cans carefully so that you can close them tightly after each use.
- Wrap cookies and crackers in plastic bags, and keep them in tight containers.
- Empty opened packages of sugar, dried fruits and nuts into screw-top jars or airtight cans to protect them from pests.
- Inspect all food containers for signs of spoilage before use.

Appendix E
SURVIVING AN EARTHQUAKE IN
YOUR CAR!
From the American Red Cross

You may be in your car when an earthquake occurs. Here is some information you need to be prepared.

- Bring your car to a halt as safely as possible.
- Avoid stopping near or under overpasses, buildings, and utility wires.
- Stay calm and remain in your car.
- Set parking brake and turn off motor.
- When shaking stops, proceed cautiously, if possible.
- Avoid bridges and other elevated structures that might have been damaged and could be further damaged by aftershocks.
- If a power line has fallen across your car, stay in your car. Wait to be rescued. DO NOT GET OUT.

You may be forced to spend many hours in or near your car before it can be moved or before you are rescued and given transportation to a safe location.

Keep a 72-hour kit in your car.
- Bottled water
- Non-perishable food, store in sealable plastic bags
- First aid kit and book
- Flashlight—fresh and spare batteries and bulb
- Fire extinguisher—A-B-C Type
- Extra clothes, jeans, sweater, blanket
- Short rubber hose—for siphoning
- Sturdy shoes or boots for walking
- Tools—screwdriver, pliers
- An extra pair of glasses
- Essential medication
- Local maps
- Flares

For more information contact your local American Red Cross.

DETAILED OUTLINE

Appendices

PREPARATION ACTION PLAN

NO	ITEM	APPROX COST	INDIVIDUAL RESPONSIBLE	DATE DUE	DATE DONE

PREPARATION ACTION PLAN

NO	ITEM	APPROX COST	INDIVIDUAL RESPONSIBLE	DATE DUE	DATE DONE

PREPARATION UPDATE MAINTENANCE PLAN

NO	ITEM TO CHECK	DATE LAST CHECKED	INDIVIDUAL RESPONSIBLE	DATE DUE	DATE DONE

PREPARATION UPDATE MAINTENANCE PLAN

NO	ITEM TO CHECK	DATE LAST CHECKED	INDIVIDUAL RESPONSIBLE	DATE DUE	DATE DONE

HOME EMERGENCY ACTION PLAN

NO	ACTIVITY	PERSON ASSIGNED	DATE PRACTICED	DATE PRACTICED

HOME EMERGENCY ACTION PLAN

NO	ACTIVITY	PERSON ASSIGNED	DATE PRACTICED	DATE PRACTICED

SELF-RELIANT LIVING
By James and Jeani McKeever

This useful book tells you *step-by-step how to make a transition from the city to a small town, a rural community or property in the country, or even to be more self-reliant in the city.* This is not a theoretical book; this is *real life-knowledge!* Learn how to build a self-reliant home, whether in the city or in the country. Gain knowledge about other important considerations, such as electrical generation, sewage and waste disposal, and having a greenhouse, a garden, a vineyard, an orchard and animals. *A "how to" book you won't want to be without!*

Omega Publications   BC-125
P.O. Box 4130
Medford, OR 97501

Please send me _____ copies of the book *Self-Reliant Living* ($19.99 each). Or _____ copies of the book *Self-Reliant Living* and *The Self-Reliant Living Workbook* (special combination price $69.00). Enclosed is $_____.

Name _____

Address _____

City, State_____ Zip _____

SELF-RELIANT WORKBOOK

The Self-Reliant Workbook is a companion book to go with *Self-Reliant Living*. This is a working book in the form of a looseleaf, three ring binder with divider tabs for subjects such as: construction ideas, orchards, solar energy, poultry, water supply, sheep and goats, gardening, vineyards, greenhouses, farm equipment, wind and water energy, hunting and trapping, fish farming, septic systems and preserving food.

It includes some excellent articles from other sources on many of these subjects. Also included are a whole host of photographs and diagrams of how the McKeevers actually did things on the ranch. A picture *is* worth a thousand words! This was the last book written by James McKeever, the late Founder of Omega Ministries, and it contains a wealth of practical knowledge from his many years of experience. This information can be invaluable to you in becoming more self-reliant.

— — — — — — — — — — — — — — — — — — —

Omega Publications   BC-125
P.O. Box 4130
Medford, OR 97501

Please send me _____ copies of *The Self-Reliant Workbook* ($59.99 each). Enclosed is $_____.

Name _____

Address _____

City, State _____ Zip _____

ORDER FORM

Omega Publications & Videos   BC-125
P.O. Box 4130
Medford, OR 97501   Email: omegapublications@juno.com

☐   I would like to order the following **videos** ($19 each)

_____ *Canning is Fun*—Jeani McKeever-Harroun
_____ *Dehydrating Made Easy*—Jeani McKeever-Harroun
_____ *Gardening Essentials*—Dr. Barbara Fair
_____ *Nutrition Update: It's Not Too Late*—
    Dr. Mary Ruth Swope and Jeani M.-Harroun
_____ *A Practical Guide to Nutrition*—Jeani M.-Harroun
_____ *Practical Preparation*—Dr. James McKeever
_____ *Preparation For Emergencies*—Wadsworths
_____ *A Total Approach to Health*—Jeani M.-Harroun
_____ *Using Nutrition As Medicine*—
    Dr. Mary Ruth Swope
_____ *Vital Food Storage*—Dr. Barbara Fair

_____ *The Y2K Family Preparedness Video Series*
    (8 hours plus the *Y2K Preparedness National
    Yellow Pages*—$159, post. paid)—various speakers

NOTE: Please add $3 for shipping and handling for each video.
    Prices are subject to change without notice.

Charge to: ☐ Visa   ☐ Mastercard   ☐ Discover

Card No. _____ Expires _____

Signature _____

Name _____

Address _____

City, State _____ Zip _____

ORDER FORM AND
INFORMATION REQUEST

Omega Publications & Videos   BC-125
P.O. Box 4130
Medford, OR 97501   Email: omegapublicaitons@juno.com

☐   Please send me information about other books and videos
    by Dr. James McKeever or Jeani McKeever-Harroun.

☐   I would like to order the following **books**:

_____   *Foods That Heal* ($20)—Maureen Salaman
_____   *The Future Revealed* ($10.99)—
        Dr. James McKeever
_____   *Self-Reliant Living*—($19.99)
        Dr. James McKeever and Jeani McKeever-Harroun
_____   *Self-Reliant Living Workbook*—($59.99)
        Dr. James McKeever and Jeani McKeever-Harroun

NOTE: Please add $3 for shipping and handling for each book.
      Prices are subject to change without notice.

Charge to: ☐ Visa   ☐ Mastercard   ☐ Discover

Card No. _____ Expires _____

Signature _____

Name _____

Address _____

City, State _____ Zip _____